Relational Realms

Relational Realms

Helping Educators Navigate and Cultivate Healthy Schoolhouse Relationships

Diana Wandix-White and Vicki G. Mokuria

ROWMAN & LITTLEFIELD
Lanham • Boulder • New York • London

Published by Rowman & Littlefield
An imprint of The Rowman & Littlefield Publishing Group, Inc.
4501 Forbes Boulevard, Suite 200, Lanham, Maryland 20706
www.rowman.com

86-90 Paul Street, London EC2A 4NE

British Library Cataloguing in Publication Information Available

Library of Congress Cataloging-in-Publication Data

Names: Wandix-White, Diana, author. | Mokuria, Vicki G., author.
Title: Relational realms: helping educators navigate and cultivate healthy
    schoolhouse relationships / Diana Wandix-White and Vicki G. Mokuria.
Description: Lanham, Maryland: Rowman & Littlefield, [2023] | Includes
    bibliographical references.
Identifiers: LCCN 2022054461 (print) | LCCN 2022054462 (ebook) |
    ISBN 9781475867206 (Cloth: acid-free paper) | ISBN 9781475867213
    (Paperback: acid-free paper) | ISBN 9781475867220 (eBook)
Subjects: LCSH: Interaction analysis in education. | Teacher-student relationships. |
    Parent-teacher relationships.
Classification: LCC LB1034 .W355 2023 (print) | LCC LB1034 (ebook) |
    DDC 371.102/2—dc23/eng/20221206
LC record available at https://lccn.loc.gov/2022054461
LC ebook record available at https://lccn.loc.gov/2022054462

♾™ The paper used in this publication meets the minimum requirements of American National Standard for Information Sciences—Permanence of Paper for Printed Library Materials, ANSI/NISO Z39.48-1992.

*For our respective children and their children and
everybody's children.*

No one is born hating another person because of the colour of his skin, or his background, or his religion. People must learn to hate, and if they can learn to hate, they can be taught to love, for love comes more naturally to the human heart than its opposite.

—Nelson Mandela

Contents

Introduction

THE ADVENTURES OF DI AND VI

Vicki and I decided to have periodic one- or two-day writing retreats to help us stay focused on our writing. We live about three and a half hours from each other, so we usually try to find a place in between. Based on our five-year friendship and several travels and adventures together, I know that when Vicki makes the arrangements, we'll be doing a modern-day, American middle-class version of roughin' it (truly an adventure!). True to form, we were booked to stay in a questionable "hotel" in a less-than-desirable part of an unfamiliar town. I suggested we meet around 9:00 or 10:00 a.m., but Vicki requested noon or 1:00 p.m. We agreed on 12:30 p.m. While en route, I called Vicki and found that she was already there. I was barely out of my neighborhood. I was immediately frustrated and questioned why we couldn't have met earlier instead of wasting half the morning. I verbalized these thoughts and Vicki said, "Girl, it is what it is now. It's all good. I'm just sitting in the parking lot." (Vicki and I are both "go with the flow" kind of people, but her flow is a bit more fluid than mine.) She calls me again and says, "Let's just meet at this coffee shop I found. I'll send you the address." As I'm attempting to change my navigation entry while driving, I feel my frustration rising, so I began to pray. I pray I won't have an attitude when I get there because we really need to focus and get some writing done, and I know we won't be able to if we're in a heightened state of dissonance due to the current situation.

Vicki called a short while later and asked if I wanted to talk through some of our writing plans while driving. I responded, "No, thank you. I need to *Woosah* for the next ten minutes. I'll see you in ten or fifteen." We both laughed and she commented, "Yes, because I can feel your irritation miles away, so you *Woosah* so that we can be productive!"

When I arrive at the coffee house, it's really a restaurant, and we get a table in a covered outside area. There are enough flies to make you think there's a dead horse ten feet away. We were both using our menus to fight the swarm (okay, maybe not a swarm, but close). Call me difficult, but I just couldn't do it. I suggest we just go to the hotel and that's when Vicki informs me she canceled the hotel because while she was sitting in the parking lot, there was some illegal solicitation going on across the street.

We found another hotel and carried our bags up to the room. Guess what? You guessed it. The keys didn't work. Once we got the keys re-coded and entered the room, there was only one king-size bed. Uh, no. Back to the front office a third time. Thank goodness; they were able to get us a room with two queens. It is now 2:00 p.m., and I've had a mimosa somewhere along the way. I'm praying, Vicki's chanting, and we're both laughing because, for us, this is far from abnormal.

We begin with this story because one of the ways we as humans connect to one another is through the stories we tell of our life experiences. Our stories hold powerful influence over our identities and how we come to know ourselves and the world around us; and when we open ourselves to the narrative of others, we open ourselves to the possibility of uncovering hidden commonalities and bridges of connection. It was through the personal narrative of a PE teacher as shared through several articles by Craig et al. (2012, 2013, 2014, 2017) and You and Craig (2015) that we first conceived relational realms.

HOW WE GOT HERE

Sometimes understanding how an idea or concept emerged helps to better understand the actual idea or concept. So, allow us to share with you how we came about relational realms.

We were both nontraditional doctoral students—older than most by at least a decade. We became "reluctant" friends who increasingly found so many things in common, in spite of our clear differences. A central place of intersectionality was and continues to be our genuine belief in the importance of educators developing and showing care and empathy for their students.

We decided to collaborate on a book chapter (Mokuria & Wandix-White, 2021, pp. 181–201). Initially, we were excited about the prospect but became increasingly less so as we juggled it, our dissertations, and other projects.

One of those other projects was a presentation proposal that was accepted for a conference in Scotland. We used that conference as an excuse to have a short adventure in Europe—visiting Paris, London, Scotland, and Ireland. In the midst of our travels, we were determined to get our book chapter done, and on the many train rides and walks, we often came back to this book chapter with which we were struggling quite a bit.

The idea of relational realms came to us during one of our walks. We had just finished presenting about some rather uncomfortable and painful aspects of childhood linked to our experiences with teachers and school leaders we believed to be less than concerned about our personal or academic success. It was an "aha!" moment for us. We could clearly see how profoundly the many ways people relate to each other impact us all in seen and unseen ways—from our past to our present, and into our future. Also, to be honest, we're both veteran English teachers who love figurative language, so *relational realms* just had a ring to it.

We spent the next several days diving into various relationships, specifically in connection to the relationship between teachers and students, and teachers and the many other people they encounter in their professional lives. In the book chapter we authored, we discuss the impact of culture on relationships, and we briefly mention Jordan et al.'s (2004) thoughts on relational competence, but we didn't include relational cultural knowing or relational competence in our first diagram of relational realms. We realize, however, that these two realms are essential to discussions of building and maintaining relationships. You'll understand why when you read those chapters.

Each relational realm illuminates the complexities of relationships and the ways in which relational interactions can result in positive or negative outcomes. We focus on relational realms to

- help teachers build and maintain relationships with students, students' families, school administrators, and peers;
- offer a shared vocabulary that allows us to speak clearly about what we're experiencing in our attempt to build and maintain relationships;

- provide a conceptual framework for researchers who want an analytical tool to study issues linked to relationships; and
- aid us all in more deeply understanding the many complicated relationships in our lives.

   The point of reading about, studying, and reflecting on relational realms is for us all to have a flexible, yet simple, tool to use whenever we feel stuck or confused in a relationship with any of the individuals in our personal or work environment.

   We believe the idea of relational realms can also be viewed as a lens to more clearly understand both the root of a relational issue and a possible pathway out of the challenges, sleepless nights, or anxiety linked to that relationship. This is especially true for those relationships that seem intractable, painful, or difficult. By using the lens of relational realms, we may be able to identify why we are having such a challenge relating to or connecting with someone. We all know we can never *change* anyone else; it's up to you to make some kind of internal shift. Using the ideas in this book can offer insight and practical strategies to work on within so that you can begin to improve or heal some of those relationships that might be difficult for you now. As Maya Angelou once said, "Do the best you can until you know better. Then when you know better, do better." We are all living and learning. Hopefully, the ideas we present about relational realms will support you to "know better" so you can "do better" as a person and professional.

   Finally, in a world full of mental and physical barriers, we need to find and/ or create bridges. We believe that the ideas we offer to you about relational realms can serve as bridges to create connections with others, especially in those circumstances that cause us the most angst. As living, thinking, breathing, caring, and curious human beings who choose not to give up easily, we must seek out or create bridges and pathways for healing. We believe relational realms will help you on your journey as an educator as you seek to nurture and support each and every student in your midst.

REFERENCES

Craig, C. J., You, J., & Oh, S. (2012). Why school-based narrative inquiry in physical education research? An international perspective. *Asia Pacific Journal of Education, 32*(3), 271–284.

Craig, C., You, J. & Oh, S. (2013). Collaborative curriculum making in the physical education vein: A narrative inquiry of space, activity and relationship. *Journal of Curriculum Studies, 45*(2), 169–197.

Craig, C. J., You, J., & Oh, S. (2014). Tensions in teacher community: Competing commitments in the teaching of US middle school physical education. *Journal of Curriculum Studies, 46*(5), 697–728.

Craig, C., You, J., & Oh, S. (2017). Pedagogy through the pearl metaphor: Teaching as a process of ongoing refinement. *Journal of Curriculum Studies, 49*(6), 757–781.

Jordan, J. V., Walker, M., & Hartling, L. M. (Eds.). (2004). *The complexity of connection: Writings from the Stone Center's Jean Baker Miller Training Institute.* The Guilford Press.

Mokuria, V. G., & Wandix-White, D. (2021). Something is a bit fishy: Wading through Helen's experiences in relational realms. In L. Asadi & C. J. Craig (Eds.), *Truth and knowledge in curriculum making* (pp. 181–202). Information Age Publishing.

You, J., & Craig, C. (2015). Narrative accounts of US teachers' collaborative curriculum making. *Sport, Education and Society, 20*(40), 501–526.

1

Relational Epistemology

Our Foundational Knowledge Base and Its Impact on Relationships

WHAT IS RELATIONAL EPISTEMOLOGY?

Weird, high-falutin, academic-sounding words can annoy us, but before you skip this chapter because it has the word "epistemology" in its title, take a deep breath and stay with us! In simplest terms, the word "epistemology" means the study or theory of knowledge. Like many words, epistemology has more than one definition, and it's the second meaning that is significant to this discussion: *epistemology is the investigation of what distinguishes justified belief from opinion* (as listed in Google Dictionary). Why is it significant? Because *relational* epistemology identifies knowing as a process through which individuals develop a pseudo-relationship with others based on socially constructed insight and/or superficial experiences with individuals or groups who create for the individual a synecdoche representing the entire group. In other words, relational epistemology compels us to look at how we've formed our knowledge base about others and demands that we deconstruct judgments and conclusions we've made based on shallow or limited interactions. This is an extremely important exercise for all of us, but especially for those of us in positions of authority whose relational generalizations have the power to significantly impact the trajectory of the lives of those under our perceived control. We're talking about managers and supervisors, police officers, doctors, lawyers, and yes, teachers!

EDUCATORS AND RELATIONAL EPISTEMOLOGY

When teachers fail to examine their own relational epistemology, it can be very dangerous for the teacher-student relationship. Imagine the teacher who has had a few athletes in class, and those athletes have been boisterous, distracted on Fridays because they're ready for the big game, and they get the whole class off-task by asking seemingly relevant questions designed to change the direction of conversation and avoid work. (Yes, that's a stereotyped description, but that's the point.) After this experience with athletes, the teacher may become anxious anytime her class roster includes student athletes. A negative attitude is set before the student ever enters the classroom. Does the teacher have a justified belief about *all* athletes? Or a biased opinion based on limited interaction?

We need for you to truly grasp the gravity of relational epistemology, so let's look at some non-school related examples just to make sure we really understand how relational epistemologies can be quite harmful when left unexamined. We'll start out light. Think about how many people you know or have heard of who don't like doctors. Okay, so when you were little, a person wearing a white coat, sitting in a cold, funny-smelling room, jammed a popsicle stick down your throat and then stuck you somewhere sensitive with a sharp, pointy thing. Your parents called that person *doctor*, and ever since then you've just had a bad vibe about those types of people. Or more seriously, through personal experience or some form of media, you witnessed law enforcement do harm instead of good, and due to that socially constructed knowledge, you don't trust police officers. Or you're the police officer who has had one or two bad experiences with men of color, so now you're a bit jumpy and much more aggressive when you encounter those guys. One more: you manage or own a store and you've had a few teenagers come in and steal from you. Now, anytime one of those kids comes into your store, you dial 9 and 1 and follow them around with the phone in your hand and your thumb ready to hit that second 1. You see, if we allow our process of knowing and knowledge development to end prematurely at the stage in which our understanding is superficial (especially if that understanding was developed under adverse circumstances and is therefore negative) and then we apply that superficial understanding to all other similar people or situations, then we will never grow and develop that understanding beyond the deformity or stunted growth it inevitably suffered during its premature birth.

Bottom line, try really hard not to allow a not-so-great experience with one person or student to dictate how you think, feel, or interact with other people or students who have similar characteristics; never stop interrogating your own knowledge; always be open to changing your ideas when confronted with new information; and be willing to acknowledge the fact that your positionality can bias your epistemology.

HOW EPISTEMOLOGY IMPACTS BOTH HOW AND WHAT WE TEACH AND LEARN

So, we're going to take a detour for a bit. It may seem like the detour is less about relational epistemology and more about epistemology in general, and it sort of is, but it is only when we stop and deeply consider what knowledge is and how we develop our knowledge base and, thus, our understanding of the world that we truly grow and expand our understanding of ourselves and others. It's all linked to epistemology.

The study of theories of knowledge, or epistemology, is oftentimes linked to Plato and Socrates and the Greek philosophers who spent a great deal of time asking philosophical questions about the very nature of life and the human condition. While the roots of these ideas come from philosophy, those of us committed to education can benefit from dipping our toes into the waters of the philosophers' seas of ideas. Let's start with a powerful metaphor called the "allegory of the cave." You may have been introduced to it at some point in your life, possibly in a high school English class or a college philosophy course.

Plato introduces the "Allegory of the Cave" in *The Republic*. Here's the scene: below the ground is a cave with about four or five prisoners sitting down with their arms and legs chained to a half wall behind them. Behind the wall is a huge fire that lights the cave. Between the wall and the fire, some men are walking back and forth holding puppets to represent such items as horses, birds, or other similar objects. With the fire behind the puppeteers, the objects appear as shadows on the walls of the cave. The chained prisoners are facing the cave walls and watch the shadows projected in front of them (see figure 1.1).

Figure 1.1   Plato's Cave. *An Illustration of the "Allegory of the Cave" from Plato's* Republic, 2018, Wikimedia Commons. (https://commons.wikimedia.org/wiki/File:An_Illustration_of _The_Allegory_of_the_Cave,_from_Plato%E2%80%99s_Republic.jpg). CC4.0.

They engage in discussions about what they believe the images are or might mean, based on their *limited experiences and opinions* as chained prisoners in a cave. One of the prisoners is freed and makes the ascent out of the cave.

Due to the brightness of the sun, the prisoner who is ascending into the daylight is almost blinded as he leaves the cave; with time, his eyes become accustomed to the sunlight. As the freed prisoner looks around at life outside the cave, he has one realization after another. He sees birds flying overhead, horses galloping, and notices that shadows are a mere casting of real objects and can distort or shift the reality of that entity. The freed prisoner recognizes the limitations of being chained in a cave and having a very constricted and limited view of life and the world and, therefore, seeing things not the way they truly are. This "awakening" is overwhelming to him because he realizes how he and all his friends have been deluded in their limited understanding of life. They've only been able to focus on the shadows and develop opinions based on their distorted perceptions; thus, they have formed erroneous beliefs without ever realizing it.

As we consider our relational epistemology, we are often like the chained, involuntarily blinded and misled prisoners whose unquestioned internal biases were created and stoked by the fires of people who hid behind walls and tricked us into accepting shadows as reality. The shadows are all the deficit thinking we internalize about our students, ourselves, and others (especially those "others" who are different from us). They are our opinions that are based on the pictures various media forms place in front of us, warped by the experiences those who are "chained down" with us have projected onto us, and rooted in the fears our minds have conjured up within us. When we don't break free of the chains and expose ourselves to new light and new realities, we limit ourselves and remain stuck in the shadows; we essentially restrict ourselves to one way of seeing and believing everything we know. Think about how dangerous that is. We would never grow, change, adapt, develop, or create anything new.

So why did we think it important to fill a whole page or two telling you about Plato's allegory of the cave? Well, here's the really big aha . . . ready? As educators, we need to be the ones to escape the cave!

Oh, and we didn't finish the story. After some point, the freed prisoner is compelled to go back into the cave and share with the other prisoners what he has experienced, discovered, and learned. Once we free ourselves and investigate the world outside of our limited exposure, we owe it to our students to help them examine the nature, origin, and scope of their knowledge and aid them in expanding their scope of knowledge and rationality of beliefs. The goal is not a new indoctrination or new chains in a new cave. The goal is to cultivate critical thinking and impassioned humanity so that students acknowledge and respect that their way of thinking is not axiomatic and that differing views are not a reason for broken friendships, isolation, bullying, or war.

For Plato, it would seem, the role of education is to support us to "see" life clearly. For each one of us, the "chains" in our lives are those ideas and beliefs developed during our socialization processes that quite possibly have contributed to us (mis)understanding ourselves, others, or life in general. Our unexamined biases are a result of our socialization linked to those chains, and true education can help free us in ways we are not always aware of. It's almost like the "relationship" we have with celebrities. It's like reading a book written about Beyoncé and judging her based on information in that book, or feeling like you *know* her based on what you've read. Yet, you've never met her, never had a conversation with her, never found out the "what made you do this or say that."

When we recognize that our epistemological worldview is a result of how we have been socialized (or the hints and shaded views of reality we read in our Beyoncé book), we also recognize the same is true for others. But, this part is key: it is no easy task to do the deep inner work and consider who we are and how we came to believe and know the many ideas and values we currently embrace. It's not easy to move from the safe place on the couch with the characters in the book, or from the familiarity of the cave, to engage with the actual people and put the shadows behind us. Yet, this kind of deep inner reflection is precisely what is needed if we are to recognize our fundamental epistemological worldview, or how we came to know what we consider to be true about ourselves, others, life, and the world.

HOW TO BEGIN THE INNER WORK OF UNDERSTANDING OUR OWN EPISTEMOLOGY

Within the other relational realms discussed throughout this book, we offer concrete examples, activities, and reflection exercises to help you get started on the inner work of understanding your own epistemology. The questions below, however, may serve to stimulate this process and encourage you to consider some aspects of your foundational knowledge base and challenge taken-for-granted assumptions you may have come to embrace. Though some uncomfortable thoughts might bubble up as you ponder these questions, lean into what you discover; be honest with yourself and write down your thoughts.

1. Consider some of your earliest memories and what you heard adults in your life say about people different from your family—different religions, races, economic status, and so on. What kinds of things were said? Were others different from your family laughed at or spoken of in derogatory ways? How do you remember feeling or what do you remember thinking when you heard such talk?

2. Consider some of your earliest memories about views on the roles of men and women. What kinds of comments and statements do you remember about expectations for men and women?

3. Consider ways you were taught to act toward other people. Were elders honored and respected/revered? Did your family make fun of or joke about elders?

4. How did your family view children and their roles in the family?

5. What were some things you remember from an early age about how "success" was defined? Who were people you remember that your family looked up to and respected? What was it about those people they respected?

6. What do you remember were ideas, topics, or concepts that were considered "taboo" and that no one could ever talk about? Why was it so hard to talk about such topics?

7. What were some things from your earliest memory that you were taught were "good" or "bad?"

8. What happened within your upbringing when anyone questioned some views or ideas? How did your family deal with any questions that did not align with their beliefs?

REFERENCES

Mokuria, V. G., & Wandix-White, D. (2021). Something is a bit fishy: Wading through Helen's experiences in relational realms. In L. Asadi & C. J. Craig (Eds.), *Truth and knowledge in curriculum making* (pp. 181–202). Information Age Publishing.

Moll, Luis C. (2015). Tapping into the 'hidden' home and community resources of students. *Kappa Delta Pi Record, 51*(3), 114–117. doi: 10.1080/00228958.2015.1056661.

Plato (1937). *The dialogues of Plato*. (B. Jowett, Trans.). Random House. (Original work published ca. 375 BCE)

Thayer-Bacon, Barbara J. (1993). Caring and its relationship to critical thinking. *Educational Theory, 43*(3), 323–340.

4edges. (2018). *An Illustration of the Allegory of the Cave from Plato's Republic* [Illustration]. Wikimedia Commons. https://commons.wikimedia.org/wiki/File:An_Illustration_of_The_Allegory_of_the_Cave,_from_Plato%E2%80%99s_Republic.jpg

2

Relational Knowledge

What We Bring to Our Relationships

WHAT IS RELATIONAL KNOWLEDGE?

So, now that we've talked about the process, or *how* basic relational knowledge is formed through our epistemological foundations, let's talk about the subsequent epistemic justifications we make to rationalize—or justify—what has been ingrained in us as undeniable truths about the people, places, and things with which we are connected.

How we acquire our knowledge about being in a relationship with others greatly impacts what knowledge we accept as factual. These simple "facts" that we accept as relational truths represent our relational knowledge. Consider our Beyoncé book again—we can have knowledge of someone without knowing that someone. Let's look at it from another angle: our epistemic justification says, "Hey, I have this knowledge, and I have good reason to believe it to be true." For example, you were told as a child that Rottweilers are mean dogs, and you know this to be true because one bit you when you were ten years old. The problem is that one Rottweiler bit you. There are an estimated 1.2 million Rottweilers in the United States; the vast majority have never been reported to bite anyone. But you have "proven" to be true this previously accepted idea in your mind that Rottweilers are mean because of a single experience.

Our relational knowledge consists of the apparent facts and information we glean through beliefs and ideas ingrained in us by others and our surface-level interactions with those others. We may have peeked over Plato's wall, but we're still keeping our distance as we take in all that we see around us. In essence, relational knowledge occupies that space between our relational epistemology and all the other relational realms we experience, except relational dissonance which often results when we don't move beyond basic relational knowledge of others toward a true understanding of the person as an individual human being.

Unfortunately, most of us do not question our relational knowledge; and yet it is this relational knowledge that guides us in how we treat others, encourages us to connect with or remain disconnected from others, and motivates us to build walls or build bridges between self and others.

RELATIONAL KNOWLEDGE AND TEACHERS CONNECTING

Are you able to imagine how a teacher's relational knowledge can be detrimental to a student's overall growth and development if the teacher remains stagnant and unwilling to challenge his or her own beliefs and ideas? None of us like to admit that we do judge others by their looks or socioeconomic status, so this example may make you a tad uncomfortable. Imagine you've prepared your classroom for a new school year. The room has been thoroughly cleaned, facilities have put a new coat of paint on the walls, your whiteboard is shiny, and your Glade PlugIn has the room smelling like a fresh summer breeze. As you welcome your students into the classroom, you notice a student whose personal hygiene habits are clearly not in line with what you believe is appropriate. The student's fingernail and toenails are long and seemingly rarely cleaned; you notice this because he wears flip-flops and you have a hard time *not* noticing the long, dirty toenails. You're grossed out by his constant head scratching and picking at his sun burned skin. You also notice an unpleasant odor. Based on your Westernized cultural aspects of cleanliness, you're having a very hard time looking at or being near this student, let alone building a relationship with him. Your unchallenged belief that physically dirty people are lazy, disease-ridden, and undesirable causes you to either avoid, or worse, be unkind to this student.

Furthermore, you're probably thinking that this student needs to be referred to a counselor or a social worker because his parents are likely neglecting him. But did you know that hygiene norms are not necessarily universal? And what if you found out that your student comes from a farming family, and he's a bit dirty in the morning because he doesn't have time to get cleaned up after helping out on the farm early in the morning. Would this new knowledge help you shift your heart from rejecting your student to respecting your student?

If we remain stuck in our basic relational knowledge and refuse to consider new information and new ways of seeing others, ourselves, and the world around us, we run the risk of not only stunting our own growth but also isolating and dehumanizing those individuals who don't fit neatly into our preconceived notions.

Here's another brief example. It's the beginning of the year and you have a new co-worker. She's the same age, gender, and race as you; she's heterosexual and seems to share your religious beliefs; she appears to be middle- to upper-middle class and is dedicated to her students, just like you are. You find out that she is going through a rough divorce. You decide to befriend her and lend your support. During your first lunch together, she tells you her husband is divorcing her because she made a horrible mistake and cheated on him. Your relational knowledge that says she is deserving of your support and sympathy because she is so similar to you is now causing you to reassess because your relational knowledge also tells you that only an immoral and untrustworthy person is unfaithful to their spouse.

Building relationships with your students and colleagues will be difficult if you're unwilling to revisit those "simple facts" that we accept as relational truths.

RELATIONAL KNOWLEDGE AND TEACHERS TEACHING

As educators, our relational knowledge doesn't only impact how we connect with the people in our work environment; it also influences how we teach the curriculum. Following is an example of what we mean.

Some of us may remember the story we learned in school about Columbus and how most in his day thought the world was flat, but Columbus didn't believe it; he thought the earth was round. Based on this, he convinced the king and queen of Spain to let him sail to the New World, which ultimately landed him on islands in North America where he "discovered Indians." You may have learned the rhyme, "In fourteen hundred ninety-two, Columbus sailed the ocean blue" and colored or identified the boats he used—the *Niña* the *Pinta*, and the *Santa Maria*. This is "inert knowledge" that stays in the attics of our minds for the most part, but that we can access whenever we need it, which is hardly ever. For the history buffs among us, there was so, so, so much more to Columbus' story and how he treated the Taíno Indigenous people who lived on the island he encountered. Yet, the relational knowledge we have collectively accepted for centuries barely mentions the Taínos. It has only been recently that history buffs and scholars have sought to present "troublesome knowledge" about Columbus, resulting in some US cities changing "Columbus Day" to "Indigenous People Day." A small, but significant, shift in our foundational relational knowledge occurs when "new" knowledge helps us understand our shared version of reality from another perspective. Botha et al. (2021) make the following statement about this type of decolonization of relational knowledge:

> By mobilizing the idea of relational knowledge to guide an anticolonial
> critique, we arrive at a counterhegemonic knowledge-making model. The
> three senses in which knowledge is relational thus work together, locating
> knowledge making in local relations among actors, artifacts, and places and
> so in local identities forged by histories and negotiations of power. By shaping
> these relationships, we can systematically pursue an agenda of epistemological
> diversification. (p. 54)

We develop knowledge through shared information and experience, and a school's curriculum impacts us by serving as windows or mirrors for us all. Emily Style (1988/1996) uses the metaphor of curriculum as windows and/ or mirrors, noting "the connection between eyesight and insight" [and that] "no student acquires knowledge in the abstract; learning is always personal" (p. 1). Our ideas about connecting and relating to others are socially constructed over time. If we don't move past that socially constructed knowledge anchored within us through superficial relationships or curriculum, we lose the opportunity to form fresh and new connections with each and every person and move beyond mere relational knowledge.

Oh, and the story of Columbus reminds us of another cool, fun fact reason why it's important to revisit and reflect upon our assumptions resulting from our relational knowledge. This is also for those who want some science to support what we're saying. Scientists say that information that's repeated more than once is easier for our brains to process and that it's because of something called the illusory truth effect. The more times we hear something, the quicker our brains can process it. So even if we know a statement is false at first, each time we hear it, it becomes more familiar to us; and when our brain says, "hey, I've heard that one before," we tend to believe it a little more with every repetition. It's related to the phenomena known as knowledge neglect, where our brain gets lazy, stops fact checking, and just accepts what's easiest to understand, even if we once knew that it wasn't true at all (brain games).

CHALLENGING RELATIONAL KNOWLEDGE THROUGH OTHER TYPES OF KNOWLEDGE

Scholars, such as Perkins (1999) as well as Meyer and Land (2003), recognize many other kinds of knowledge, one being troublesome knowledge. Troublesome knowledge is the knowledge that unsettles us and causes us to rethink some ideas we have long held on to. It's the troublesome knowledge that serves to push us to consider questioning ideas we may have never before thought to doubt or question. Ultimately, troublesome knowledge forces us within and may lead us to consider another way to see and understand ourselves, how we see the world, and the viewpoints or perspectives of others (Barradell & Kennedy-Jones, 2015; Hill et al., 2016). Troublesome knowledge can serve as a gateway to a new way of thinking about ourselves and others. Possibly, troublesome knowledge can be seen as a threat because it helps us think critically about important ideas, and this is why some state legislators want to control some of the topics teachers teach, especially history and social studies.

Another important form of knowledge, especially for teachers, is termed "funds of knowledge" (Moll et al., 1992; Moll, 2019). The funds of knowledge consist of all the experiences, wisdom, and knowledge within families and their cultures that students bring with them when they step into schools and classrooms. Teachers can find creative ways to draw on families' funds of knowledge and encourage parents to engage with all the students in their classrooms. For example, a parent or grandparent might have a specific skill or talent they can share with students. By inviting the family member to share something from their cultural or familial fund of knowledge, students can learn to value and appreciate each other—while also linking the activity to a topic the teacher might cover anyway. Familial or cultural funds of knowledge are oftentimes underutilized sources of knowledge.

In addition to the kinds of knowledge mentioned above, scholars such as Freema Elbaz (1991) and Jana Krátká (2015) write extensively about teacher knowledge, which they propose is deeply personal and mostly tacit—the kind of knowledge hidden under the radar. For Elbaz (1991), teacher knowledge "is nonlinear; it has a holistic, integrated quality; it is at least partly patterned or organized; and it is imbued with personal meaning" (p. 11). From her research on the topic of teacher knowledge, teachers' stories are of particular value and importance. Ultimately, "to understand teachers, we need to understand each teacher's personal practical knowledge, his/her embodied, narrative, moral, emotional, and relational knowledge as it is expressed in practice" (Clandinin et al., 2006, p. 172). This perspective of relational knowledge requires us to listen to teachers' stories in order to explore and examine how teachers view their lives and experiences and how they view and treat students; in this way, we gain insight into teachers' relational knowledge.

DECOLONIZING RELATIONAL KNOWLEDGE

Tlostanova and Mignolo (2012) explore how we can decolonize the knowledge linked to epistemicide (the "killing" of others' foundational knowledge/ideas) and colonization, believing that "racism, in the final analysis, rests on the control of knowledge/understanding" (p. 56). Racism ultimately takes root in relational knowledge that is never "troubled" or "questioned." Linked to racism is the historical fact that during World War II, the very first people killed in villages overtaken by Nazis were the teachers. Why was that? The Nazis wanted to control the knowledge students learned, and in order to do that, they needed to kill the teachers whose academic and relational knowledge did not align with theirs. This was because "all teachers and professors [in Nazi Germany] had to belong to a Nazi Teacher Organization and take an oath 'to be loyal and obedient to Adolf Hitler'" (Connecticut State Department of Education, 1981, p. 51). Such is the power of relational knowledge and why we must be willing to be open to move beyond it into relational knowing.

Ultimately, we must take responsibility for our relational knowledge as uncomfortable as that might be. Why is some knowledge in our schools "valued," while other knowledge is dismissed or discounted? Why do so many of us struggle to simultaneously honor and respect everyone's knowledge? The answer to this might be in this quote from James Baldwin: "We can disagree and still love each other unless your disagreement is rooted in my oppression and denial of my humanity and right to exist." Does the relational knowledge we have about each and every student involve supporting them and lifting them up? Or is the relational knowledge we have developed over time affected and infected by unexamined biases that impact how we treat some of our students? These questions require us to engage in some honest self-reflection.

We can see that relational knowledge emerges from our collective shared understanding of life and the world. For example, Thayer-Bacon (2010) writes that "when we understand that we are one with the universe, then we can begin to understand how connected we are as knowers, not only to each other, but to our products as well, our knowledge" (p. 17). Just as the source of our problems AND the solutions to our problems are within us, it is also true that how we see and treat others with either a positive or negative lens emerges from within us in the form of our relational knowledge.

A key point about relational knowledge is that it consists of the "brick and mortar" of our thoughts about how we relate to other people. It is the knowledge we carry around with us from our past up until the present moment. Sometimes we question why we said or did something, and at other times we react to others automatically in ways we have been taught or conditioned to do over time—hardly ever thinking twice about it. Do we greet others warmly and with smiles, or do we barely acknowledge others? How do we greet our colleagues and students in the morning? In whatever way we answer this, it is most likely connected to our relational knowledge about ways to interact with others in the morning. Kenneth Gergen is a social psychologist who has devoted much of his life to studying and understanding relational knowledge and relational ways of being in the world.

According to Gergen (2009), knowledge is created relationally and becomes accepted as "truth" or "fact," and it is rarely, if ever, questioned.

As previously mentioned, in schools, most of us have come to accept the curriculum presented to us all our lives as indisputable facts that students must learn in order to function and operate within our world. Gergen (2009), however, suggests this:

> Rather, let us view what we take to be *knowledge as an outcome of relational processes.* Through co-action people generate a world of the real. Within a tradition of relationship a particular discourse may be counted as "knowledge," certain people as "knowledgable," and certain practices as "knowledge generating." Knowledge acquires its aura by virtue of its contribution to what is valued within the community. (p. 204–205)

Gergen reiterates that all knowledge emerges from a relational process. The last point in the above quote is key because he emphasizes that the knowledge that ultimately "counts" and "acquires its aura" is what the community values. What about a society or world that has very different ideas and values about "what counts?" How do we collectively "decide" on the knowledge that is "sacred," taught, and valued? Oftentimes, the knowledge that is valued emerges from a group that has economic or political power and that group may seek to impose on everyone its ideas about the knowledge that "counts." This applies to all the various forms of knowledge, including relational knowledge and how we respond to and treat each other.

There is nothing we can do to change the past and how we treated others or how we have been treated. To make substantive changes in any of our relationships requires dialogue, and teachers can support a dialogical process in their classrooms by creating spaces for safe and respectful exchange.

To accomplish this, Donahue-Keegan (2021) suggests that "building relational trust is foundational to establishing psychological safety, which is an essential prerequisite for authentic sharing, learning, and development within groups" (p. 109). Teachers can be the torch-bearers for creating a world where multiple perspectives, values, and views are equally embraced and respected by creating classroom spaces grounded in relational trust. In this way, students can feel safe to step beyond their relational knowledge and consider a wide range of ideas and points of view as they interact and cocreate a fresh way of engaging and learning about and from each other. We have to remember that all of our current relational knowledge is totally from the past. However, when we consider the possibility of a future we can create beyond any wounds of the present or past, we can step into relational knowing, which is a doorway to new possibilities.

REFERENCES

Barradell, S., & Kennedy-Jones, M. (2015). Threshold concepts, student learning and curriculum: Making connections between theory and practice. *Innovations in Education & Teaching International, 52*(5), 536–545. doi: 10.1080/14703297.2013.866592.

Botha, L., Griffiths, D., & Prozesky, M. (2021). Epistemological decolonization through a relational knowledge-making model. *Africa Today, 67*(4), 51–72. https://www.muse.jhu.edu/article/794677.

Clandinin, D. J., Huber, J., Huber, M., Orr, A. M., Pearce, M., & Steeves, P. (2006). *Composing diverse identities: Narrative inquiries into the interwoven lives of children and teachers.* Routledge.

Connecticut State Department of Education. (1981, March). Man's inhumanity to man: A case in point: The Nazi Holocaust.: A resource for Connecticut teachers, grades 7–12. https://eric.ed.gov/?id=ED201586.

Donahue-Keegan, D. (2021). Social-emotional learning and value-creating education: Synergistic possibilities for cultivating hope and joy in education. In I. Nuñez & J. Goulah (Eds.), *Hope and joy in education: Engaging Daisaku Ikeda across curriculum and context* (pp. 104–113). Teachers College Press.

Elbaz, F. (1991). Research on teacher's knowledge: The evolution of a discourse. *Journal of Curriculum Studies, 23*(1), 1–19. doi: 10.1080/002202791023010

Gergen, K. L. (2009). *Relational being: Beyond self and community.* Oxford University Press.

Hill, J., Thomas, G., Diaz, A., & Simm, D. (2016). Borderland spaces for learning partnership: Opportunities, benefits and challenges, *Journal of Geography in Higher Education, 40*(3), 375–393. http://researchspace.bathspa.ac.uk/7268/1/7268.pdf.

Krátká, J. (2015). Tacit knowledge in stories of expert teachers. *Procedia- Social and Behavioral Sciences, 171*, 837–846. doi: 10.1016/j.sbspro.2015.01.19.

Meyer, J., & Land, R. (2005). Threshold concepts and troublesome knowledge (2): Epistemological considerations and a conceptual framework for teaching and learning. *Higher Education, 49*(3), 373–388. doi: 10.1007/s10734-004-6779-5.

Moll, L., Amanti, C., Neff, D., & Gonzalez, N. (1992). Funds of knowledge for teaching: Using a qualitative approach to connect homes and classrooms. *Theory into Practice, 31*(2), 132–141. doi: 10.1080/00405849209543534.

Moll, L. C. (2019). Elaborating funds of knowledge: Community-oriented practices in international contexts. *Literacy Research: Theory, Method, and Practice, 68*, 130–138. doi: 10.1177/2381336919870805.

Perkins, D. (1999). The many faces of constructivism. *Educational Leadership, 57*(3), 6–11.

Simon, M. (2020, Jan. 20). Ted Danson: Fact or fiction (Season 8, Episode 2) In T. Marquess –D. Cutforth, T. Gorman, E. Key, K. Key, C. Kriley, J. Lipsitz, M. Renner, J. Rowley, L. Williams (Executive producers), *Brain Games*. Magical Elves Productions; National Geographic Television

Style, E. (1996). Curriculum as window and mirror. *Social Science Record.* Reprinted from *Listening for All Voices*, Oak Knoll School monograph, Summit, NJ, 1988, 1–5.

Thayer-Bacon, B. (2010). A pragmatist and feminist relational (e)pistemology. *European Journal of Pragmatism and American Philosophy, 2*(1), 1–22. doi: 10.4000/ejpap.948.

Tlostanova, M. V., & Mignolo, W. D. (2012). *Learning to unlearn: Decolonial reflections from Eurasia and the Americas.* The Ohio University Press.

3

Relational Dissonance

Its Purpose and How to Transform It

WHAT IS RELATIONAL DISSONANCE?

Relational dissonance describes the jarring, uncomfortable emotions that result from a clash of values, beliefs, ideas, or views that are rooted in staunch beliefs held by those who are in relationship with one another. Look at the individual words in the preceding sentence: *dissonance, jarring, uncomfortable, clash*. This is not a pretty stage in the relationship journey, but it can be the tunnel that opens to a beautiful landscape or one that at least has fewer thorns and bristles. But first, we have to find the tunnel and locate the portal.

If you've ever been in a relationship, you've likely had the "I thought everything was fine" experience in which one person is upset and the other is clueless. For example, because of my personal beliefs and values, I'm not a fan of excessive, unnecessary expletives (limited, unavoidable ones that slip out when you kick your baby toe on the end table and then spill the hot coffee you were carrying on the shirt you just put on for work is another story), but I have a friend who must have been a sailor in a past life. At one point I began to avoid her. Initially, she was unaware of our relational dissonance, and I was avoiding what I thought would be an awkward conversation in which I would seem prudish and she would feel like she could no longer be herself around me. Eventually, she asked what was going on, and I told her what was bothering me. Only then were we able to "go through the tunnel" and come out in a better place, each giving a little in order to retain a friendship we both valued.

Let's use this same description of relational dissonance to consider the potential for dissonance in the teacher-student relationship. We'll focus on US K–12 public schools for simplicity. The average age of teachers in US K–12 public schools is 42.7; 74 percent of them identify as female, and 72.3 percent are White/non-Hispanic. Students in these schools range from age five to nineteen, just over half of them are boys, and over 50 percent are students of color (Zippia, 2022; NCES, 2022). In addition, according to neuroscientists the human brain is not fully mature until age twenty-five. So while your mature, rational, fully conscious brain is firing on all cylinders (at least on Tuesdays), your students are struggling to function with immature, irrational, underdeveloped brains (only Monday–Wednesday, Thursday; oh, and Friday). Due to the age gap between a forty-something-year-old and a child or adolescent, as well as gender and racial contrasts, it stands to reason that there might be an occasional clash of values, beliefs, ideas, or world views. (By the way, don't take our description of your students seriously. Having over fifty collective years of K–12 experience, We know their brains are very often firing on all cylinders. Some of the most rational people we've spoken with have been high schoolers, and we've engaged with many middle schoolers who've behaved more maturely than some adults we've known.)

Another way to define relational dissonance is disharmony that emerges when one person feels in some way threatened by the other, due to power dynamics or rifts in the relationship, resulting from hurt feelings or unresolved issues. The unavoidable power dynamics between a teacher and student, teacher and administrator, or even between teacher and teacher creates a ripe opportunity for hurt feelings and unresolved issues.

Take a moment to reflect and fill in the following chart.

I hurt my student's feelings when I . . .	This issue was or was not resolved because . . .
My student hurt my feelings when s/he . . .	This issue was or was not resolved because . . .
I hurt my administrator's feelings when I . . .	This issue was or was not resolved because . . .
My administrator hurt my feelings when s/he . . .	This issue was or was not resolved because . . .
I hurt my coworker's feelings when I . . .	This issue was or was not resolved because . . .
My coworker hurt my feelings when s/he . . .	This issue was or was not resolved because . . .

At this point, we hope you can define relational dissonance and identify some instances of it occurring in your life. We especially hope you're able to recall a dissonant relationship phase in your professional life; maybe even a present one that this book can help you work through.

WHY DOES RELATIONAL DISSONANCE HAPPEN?

No two people in the world are exactly alike. That's why relational dissonance happens. Even identical twins have differences—different preferences and different desires. So, rarely is the created sound one of complete unison when two or more human beings interact. The discordant notes inevitably lead to dissonance. Also, if we review the relational dissonance definitions discussed in the previous section, we can begin to create our own list of reasons why relational dissonance occurs:

- clash of values, beliefs, ideas, or views
- people are in relationships with one another (it's inevitable!)
- hurt feelings
- power dynamics
- feelings of vulnerability
- unresolved issues

We could go on, but you get it.

More dangerous is that sometimes basic relational knowledge (see chapter 2) or relational epistemology (see chapter 1) can prompt tension, conflict, or devaluation that results in relational dissonance (Bond et al., 2014). The limited knowledge we glean about another through limited interaction or socially constructed ideas can move us to assign a monolithic story to whole groups of people. If that surface knowledge or experience has been negative, then we've judged a whole bunch of people based on our experience with one or two or maybe ten with whom we've had a bad experience. For example, Johnny Adams was in your class two years ago and his behavior helped you grow spiritually because you had to spend so much time in prayer or meditation. You taught his sister, Lisa, a few years before that and she helped you spend more time with your family because you had to take a leave of absence to regain your sanity. Now their little brother, Joey, is on your roster. You're already having heart palpitations and dry mouth and you haven't even met him.

We also know this happens when we prejudge our students and their families, school leaders, or coworkers based on language or speech patterns, physical ability, race, gender, political affiliation, religion, and so on. Relational dissonance can have devastating effects on education and can occur in various relationships: teacher-student, student-student, teacher-administrator, teacher-parent, administrator-parent, school-community, and any other way that the various stakeholders can be paired. While it's important to acknowledge and address relational dissonance in any of these relationships, it is imperative that teachers do not allow relational dissonance to negatively influence their relationship with a student.

In a popular TED talk, Rita Pierson (2013) perceptively comments that teachers who have a difficult time getting along with certain students must become great actors and actresses who never show their disdain and never give up on the student, no matter how challenging the student and that teacher-student relationship may be. It may be difficult for teachers to muddle through relational dissonance with students, but successfully traversing this realm is vital to the success of both the student and the teacher. We offer ways to do this a little further on in the chapter.

By the way, Joey turns out to be an angel.

WHAT HAPPENS IF WE JUST SIT IN RELATIONAL DISSONANCE?

Think back to a time when you experienced relational dissonance that seemed protracted and unmovable. It may be one of the experiences you listed in the chart about hurt feelings. No solution seemed to be clear, and each party appeared to have their heels dug in, knowing they were right. The dissonance becomes the central focus of the relationship, and at such times, it looks like the rupture in the relationship is all that is left. Relational dissonance can leave a large empty pit in our stomachs where there may have previously been joy, friendship, love, and laughter. But the dissonance took center stage and the spotlight is shining on the dissonance alone—obscuring all the other ways we may have previously related to that person. A multitude of reasons exist as to what happens to us if we just "sit" in our dissonance. This section explores some of those possibilities and reasons for them.

Relational dissonance is closely tied to anger and hurt, which becomes a tangled web that snares us. Carl Rogers, a famous humanistic psychologist, once worked with a client on issues of feeling desperate, hurt, and angry. In an analysis of the taped session, Moodley et al. (2000) suggest that the dialogue between Rogers and his client "were travelling towards transformation of the 'self'" (p. 362) through the anger and hurt (probably through our earlier tunnel). This is significant.

When the focus of our lives becomes only the dissonance, we are in a space within ourselves of intense discomfort and many of us have physical reactions. If we have a spiritual practice, we may pray, if that is a way to deal with problems; we may play a recording over and over in our minds about how and why we are right; we may try (usually unsuccessfully) to suppress our thoughts and feelings about the rupture; or we may lean into it, sit with it, and ask ourselves this: what lesson(s) am I to learn from this?

Sometimes—possibly due to illness, aging, trauma, or a toxic relationship—we feel we have little to no control over certain aspects of our lives. At such times, we may work hard to control what we think we can. In struggling to exert that control, especially over others or a situation, dissonance is almost certain to emerge. While it may appear that someone has wronged us because things are not going as we want them to go, the truth is that the dissonance is coming from within and our need to control something we cannot. Recognizing this can expand our capacity to have compassion for someone with whom we're experiencing dissonance or insight into our own angst and its roots. For example, I mentored a teacher who was a yeller and a legitimate control freak. If a student even looked as if he were going to move after she told him to sit still, she would yell at him and halt instruction for a few minutes while staring at him until he was stock-still. If a paper was put in the assignment tray, she'd yell about the order and have the perpetrator straighten out all the papers. If a student walked a step ahead of her on the way to the cafeteria, she'd make them all return to class and start over. After many, many discussions about childhood trauma and discipline that preserves dignity, I learned that this teacher was dealing with her own trauma. She suffered from an eating disorder and often felt she was not in control of her health. It was important for her to have complete control over some aspects of her life so she fought for that power in her classroom. Self-reflection can help us to consider what internal shifts we may need to make in order to move beyond dissonance in a relationship.

Our perception of the person or people with whom we are experiencing relational dissonance clouds our capacity to see any other perspective than our own, which usually feels and sounds like "I am clearly right; you are clearly wrong" about whatever is at the source of the dissonance. When an educator experiences relational dissonance with a student, the dissonant energy in the room is palpable, and all the other students know there is a power struggle and can feel it. The teacher may write a referral or send the student out to visit with the counselor, but these are all temporary fixes for a deeper problem. The teacher and student are manifesting a much deeper power struggle, and there is no clear winner when that happens.

If we only sit in relational dissonance and neglect to self-reflect or journey through the tunnel with the other party or parties, our bodies "keep score" and store our trauma, stress, and emotional dissonance in our limbic system (van der Kolk, 1994). Precisely for this reason, it is essential that we develop coping mechanisms and strategies to face, deal with, and overcome relational dissonance. Another personal example might provide insight into one approach. As a high school teacher several years ago, I had a class of about twenty-five students who were in the tenth grade. There was one student, Abigail (pseudonym), who seemed to derive great pleasure watching me unsuccessfully manage the class as she talked with her friend, filed her nails, or cleaned out her purse. She had an amazing capacity to get under my skin, and she was very skilled at it. I tried everything I had ever done with a student in the past: I met with her privately and discussed her behavior; I reached out to the parent for a parent-teacher conference; I sent her to speak with the counselor. And yet, the distracting and disrespectful behaviors continued unabated. Honestly, the relational dissonance I experienced with that student was never "fully" resolved. I found ways to maintain my professionalism, always treating her with kindness and respect despite what she said or did. As the saying goes, "Those who deserve our love the least need it the most." While we never truly healed from that dissonance, it was no longer the center of our relationship because I made up my mind that I would maintain a respectful and professional manner at all times.

Many years later (about eighteen), I was at a rally in the center of our city, and this same young woman, Abigail, came running up to me and called my name. She was so excited and asked, "Do you remember me?"

"Of course I do," I said. "Abigail, right? I think you were the *only* student I ever wrote a referral on," I said, laughing. We both laughed. She said, "Miss, I just want to apologize. I was terrible to you. Really terrible. But I want you to know that I was really listening to every single word you said. Now, I'm a social worker in a local nonprofit, and I'm really, really grateful you were patient with me and never gave up on me." Yes, those were her exact words. I remember it like it was yesterday.

After telling her how very proud I was of her, we each went our separate way. Abigail taught me such a valuable lesson. In the midst of relational dissonance, we must challenge ourselves to maintain our humanity. If we allow the dissonance to become the center of our lives and beings, we can be consumed by it. While paraphrased, another saying I once heard says, "even the container that holds poison will be eaten up by the poison." If we allow ourselves to hold onto anger, resentment, and dissonance, we are the ones who will suffer.

When looking at this issue on a systemic level, teachers are either complicit in reproducing collective relational dissonance or they will seek ways to challenge it. This is precisely why educators, in particular, can benefit from examining relational realms and learning ways to get beyond relational dissonance.

HOW DO WE MOVE OUT OF RELATIONAL DISSONANCE?

So, sometimes with relational dissonance, we have to sit with the discomfort of it for a while—lean into it, be with it, notice it, and be uncomfortable in it. An analogy can be found in a grain of sand within an oyster. The grain of sand serves as an irritant to the oyster, but from that grain of sand, a pearl grows within. Seeing relational dissonance in this way provides a pathway for us to grow from it. It is key to recognize that relational dissonance can be a source of tremendous growth, allowing us to develop ourselves and become more expansive people.

At some point, a decision is made to either focus on the inner source(s) of dissonance, develop understanding and compassion for the ones with whom we are experiencing dissonance, or find places of shared understanding. Ignoring the dissonance is a choice, but it usually results in negative emotions festering unhealthily.

Ultimately, the solution to moving out of relational dissonance lies within the hearts of those experiencing it. In school settings, teachers and the other adults in the schoolhouse are the professionals who hold the perceived power, and students are in positions of developmental growth and maturation. Further, as previously noted, students are more vulnerable; their brains are still developing, and they often lack the maturity and skills to navigate relational dissonance with finesse. It therefore behooves the adults in the building to learn and develop skills to support students when relational dissonance arises. Students learn far more from educators' behavior than their words, so modeling healthy relationship skills is important. The ideal approach is to foster healthy relationships with students from the beginning, but learning to do this requires the recognition of the value of healthy schoolhouse relationships. Even if an educator seeks to do this, relational dissonance may still occur, and finding ways to get beyond the dissonance is essential.

The following are suggestions on how to grow beyond relational dissonance and why each one is important. This is not a "prescribed" linear program but rather an offering of ideas that may lead to pathways beyond the dissonance:

- Acknowledge and accept responsibility for your connection to the situation, giving you the power and responsibility to change it.
- Look inward to recognize that what is going on is linked to disharmony within yourself and the other person; otherwise, you would not be affected by the problem.
- Find within yourself the capacity to have compassion for yourself and the other person, recognizing there is suffering on both sides.
- Seek a way within yourself to forgive yourself and the other person for the hurt.
- Look for ways to repair the harm that has been done.

- Reflect on how the situation could have been handled differently and what lessons to learn.
- Consider what is needed for healing and to move beyond the dissonance.
- Remind yourself of your "why" behind working with youth and in education.

First, we must do the deep self-reflective work necessary to heal and grow from relational dissonance by accepting responsibility for our role or part in the situation. When dealing with angry, hurt, or disrespectful students, this is not easy! Whether we are aware of it or not and whether it was our intention or not, our tones and/or words may have hurt someone deeply. While the student or colleague may not be able to articulate in words what exactly happened for them to feel disrespected, angry, or hurt, we often see and feel relational dissonance through others' behavior toward us.

Similarly, if there is relational dissonance between a teacher and a student's parent, the root of the dissonance could be within either party. Possibly, the parent had negative experiences with teachers in school and is projecting their own angst and unresolved pain from the past onto their child's teacher. Consider this simple phrase: "I am on your side to support your child to be successful." If a teacher cannot authentically say such a phrase to a parent, then it is up to teachers to do the deep inner work to understand their own hearts and what is blocking them from authentically caring for the student's success and well-being.

By looking inward, we can find the source of our hurt, anger, or fear. It may appear to be coming from the other person, but there is an inward link, and we must find it within ourselves. Palmer (2003) refers to this as the "pedagogy of the soul" and writes, "despite our cultural bias that all power resides in the outward, visible world, history offers ample evidence that the inward and invisible powers of the human spirit can have at least equal impact on our individual and collective lives" (p. 378). Recognizing, naming, and seeking to resolve relational dissonance is essential for our well-being, as well as for those with whom we have conflict, but we are reminded. The starting point is within ourselves.

When locked in relational dissonance, finding compassion for the root reason for your own hurt and suffering, along with the hurt and pain of the other person is essential. We glean insight about this from Ruiz (1997), who wrote in *The Four Agreements* about others who might say or do things that hurt us. Ruiz reminds us, don't take it personally, because the truth is that this person is dealing with his or her own feelings, beliefs and opinions. That person tried to send poison to you and if you take it personally, then you take that poison and it becomes yours. (p. 49)

Finding compassion for the way we respond and mustering a spirit of compassion for the person with whom we are conflicted provides a path to expand our understanding and our heart.

Linked to compassion is the challenge to forgive ourselves and the person we feel has hurt or harmed us. Ultimately, "forgiveness is an important corrective to the proclivities toward avoidance and revenge—people's typical negative responses to interpersonal transgressions, which seem to be etched deeply into the human template" (McCullough & Witvliet, 2002, p. 454). While the act of forgiveness can oftentimes be difficult, we may need to ask ourselves if—even once—we have hurt someone in the same way we are now experiencing hurt? Have we ever said or done something that was disrespectful to another? Forgiving ourselves and the other person can open a door to healing and counter that desire to seek revenge, which will only further exacerbate a painful situation.

Many schools today are considering restorative practices/restorative justice as a more compassionate and humane approach to school discipline, and we can learn much from this approach to solving problems in schools that arise from relational dissonance. Simply put,

> restorative justice seeks to reframe the way we conventionally think about wrong-doing and justice: it moves us from our preoccupation with lawbreaking, guilt and punishment towards a focus on harms, needs and obligations. Restorative justice especially emphasizes the importance of the engagement, dialogue and empowerment of those most affected by wrong-doing, encouraging a problem-solving approach. (Zohr, 2014, p. 97)

While used in schools, this approach can help all of us who seek to heal beyond relational dissonance and consider options to resolve the situation.

An Eastern adage states: "Life will keep bringing you the same lesson over and over until you learn it." When experiencing any kind of relational dissonance, it is essential to ask yourself, "What are lessons I must learn from this experience?" This simple but important question shifts the focus from blaming yourself or the other person and rather encourages you to consider what you need to learn. Otherwise, we miss a great opportunity to learn and grow in ways we cannot even imagine.

So, although relational dissonance can cause dis-ease and discomfort, it is also the potential source for immense growth and expansion. For growth to emerge from relational dissonance, healing is necessary, and if you make up your mind to overcome relational dissonance, you will need to consider what is needed for healing. Ultimately, Ikeda (2012) writes that "the power of healing exists within each of us from the very beginning" (p. 84). While we may think the dissonance will be resolved based on the actions of others, the true healing lies within us. As educators, this is elemental, and it is helpful to consider what Nuñez (2021) reminds us when she writes about "school as a place for connection and healing, and for finding the hope and joy that students need as sustenance" (p. 211). While the healing begins within, it extends beyond us and supports healing in our classrooms, our schools, and into our communities.

Most educators enter the field with a sincere love of teaching and learning, and with the hope of supporting young people in their growth. And yet, relational dissonance can function as a storm cloud or tornado that wreaks havoc. Pondering workable solutions to these seemingly intractable and painful relationships can serve to heal and repair the damage, in order to reclaim the joy of teaching.

WHAT HAPPENS WHEN WE MOVE OUT OF RELATIONAL DISSONANCE?

Remember when we said no two people in the world are exactly alike and we talked about the discordant notes? And at the opening of this chapter, remember how we talked about the harsh words used to define relational dissonance? Beginning with a Latin prefix that has negative associations, dissonance is naturally viewed as something to avoid, but musicians tell us that dissonance is always a matter of degree, rather than an all-or-nothing component of a composition. Think of two individuals as two different instruments that can learn how much more pitch they have and how many more beautiful notes they can play simply by acknowledging the tension and inner angst they stir up within one another. Sit in that awareness for a while, then recognize that the dissonance doesn't have to create an all-or-nothing relational roadblock, but instead can be a building block to higher notes. So, we can either revel in the discord or learn to play together harmoniously.

WHAT MIGHT I DO NOW?

Some may find the following suggestions to be silly. Nevertheless, many who use these techniques have found them to truly help the mind to recenter, refocus, and reimagine adversity into growth and meaning. Don't knock it till you try it!

(1) Guided visualizations. After taking several deep breaths and guiding your body to relax any tension you may feel, choose one of the following visualizations:

a) See yourself interacting with the person in a friendly, calm, and engaging manner. Continue with your deep breaths and visualize the two of you smiling, working together, and engaging in respectful ways as you interact.

b) Imagine the tension and dissonance between you and the other person as the bubbles that are one by one bursting and changing form.

c) Visualize a beautiful forest in the fall with the colors changing—bright yellow, orange, and red. Focusing on the leaves changing colors, recognize that they are in the process of letting go and falling to the ground. As you continue to breathe and focus on the beautiful fall foliage, let any anger, hurt, or resentment you feel fall to the ground.

(2) Journaling, prayer, or contemplation:

- How is this problem meeting some needs in your life?
- Where do you notice the angst or discomfort in your body when you think about this?
- Is there a reason you want to hold onto this situation?
- What would you need to do for this to change?
- How would you like to envision the outcome of this situation?

- What can you do to focus your thoughts and energy on other things that might help you grow beyond this situation?
- What are some lessons you need to learn from all this?
- Can you imagine a future where you are no longer bothered by this situation?
- What do you need for your own healing?
- How can you forgive yourself and others?
- How can you show yourself and others compassion?
- What can you do to let go of any anger, fear, or hurt?

REFERENCES

Bond, L., Lusher, D., Williams, I., & Butler, H. (2014, February). Friends or foes? Relational dissonance and adolescent psychological wellbeing. *PLoS ONE, 9*(2), e83388. doi: 10.1371/journal.pone.0083388.

Marinoff, L., & Ikeda, D. (2012). *The inner philosopher: Conversations on philosophy's transformative power.* Dialogue Path Press.

McCullough, M. E., & Witvliet, C. V. (2002). The psychology of forgiveness. In C. R. Snyder & S. J. Lopez (Eds.), *Handbook of positive psychology* (pp. 446–458). Oxford University Press.

Moodley R., Shipton, G., & Falken, G. (2000). The right to be desperate and hurt and angry in the presence of Carl Rogers: A racial/psychological identity approach. *Counselling Psychology Quarterly, 13*(4), 353–364. doi: 10.1080/713658498.

National Center for Educational Statistics. (2022). Fast facts: Back to school statistics. https://nces.ed.gov/fastfacts/display.asp?id=372.

Nuñez, I. (2021). Hope and joy, trust and faith, and poison as medicine. In I. Nunez & J. Goulah (Eds.), *Hope and joy in education: Engaging Daisaku Ikeda across curriculum and context.* Teachers College Press.

Palmer, P. (2003). Teaching with heart and soul: Reflections on spirituality in teacher education. *Journal of Teacher Education, 5*(54), 376–385. doi: 10.1177/0022487103257359.

Pierson, R. (2013, May). *Every kid needs a champion.* [Video]. TED Conferences. https://www.ted.com/talks/rita_pierson_every_kid_needs_a_champion.

Ruiz, D. M. (1997). *The four agreements: A Toltec wisdom book.* Amber Allen Publishing.

Zippia. (2022, April). Teacher demographics and statistics in the US. https://www
.zippia.com/teacher-jobs/demographics/.

Zohr, H. (2014). The art of justice: A reply to Bunilda Pali. *Restorative Justice*, *2*(1),
95–102. doi: 10.5235/20504721.2.1.95.

4

Relational Knowing

Getting to the Good Part

INTRODUCTION AND DEFINING TERMS

Relational knowing centers on the present moment and all of the infinite and kaleidoscopic ways we engage with, relate to, and interact with whatever or whoever is in front of us at this very moment, based on our cultural, biographical, psychological, emotional, and cognitive experiences we bring with us (Miller, 1990). Since relational knowing includes that moment in time when our past and present converge in a fluid way to engage with our current circumstances, seeds of possibility to create an unimagined future are planted at that moment.

In simplest terms for educators, then, relational knowing includes all that we bring to our classrooms and encounters with our students that are linked to our past experiences and knowledge. Relational knowing is a state of mind of "wide-awakeness" (Greene, 1978; Williams, 2017), in which teachers are fully present for their students and what the students' needs are to learn and grow. Beyond that, relational knowing involves taking some form of action. As educators, *how* we engage with, interact with, and relate to our students are oftentimes linked to such qualities as empathy, intuition, and care (Hollingsworth et al., 1993), which can be "felt" or experienced. Many of the teachers who seem to have that "magic" in their relationships with students recognize the primacy of relational knowing before curricular lessons can be taught. For those who believe in the transformative power of education, relational knowing is grounded in a hope-filled perspective that the possibility exists to find a way to connect with and support each and every student, regardless of past experiences.

Relational Knowing Begins Within

What does it really mean to be human? And how do we develop into human beings? Many of us have heard stories of children raised among wild animals and the challenges they faced in terms of language, physical, cognitive, and social development. If you're not familiar with such stories, you may want to explore the story of the wild boy of Aveyron. Even though these children may not have been nurtured by humans, aren't they still human? What is it that makes us human? These kinds of philosophical puzzles do not have a singular answer in the back of an imaginary book. If a baby is raised by a wild animal, a loving parent, or an abusive parent, the reality is that we all learn how to relate to the world and to others by how we have been treated by those who have raised us. Our earliest caregivers have such a huge influence on how we see ourselves, the world, and others around us, along with how we relate to every-thing. In those earliest years, we were either encouraged or punished for how we acted, and all of the love, anger, hurt, encouragement, fear, and dis/approval influenced us before we ever took those first steps to a school building.

In addition to parents, teachers, too, leave indelible impressions on us. Over the years, some teachers have inspired and encouraged us to be our best selves—pushing us forward to fulfill goals and dreams we possibly did not believe we could attain. Other teachers may have been critical or judgmental toward us, failing to see our humanity, vulnerabilities, strengths, or potential. The impact of teachers cannot be overstated. For those of us who believe in the potential of education to have a powerful and positive impact on students, we must both recognize and take action to provide the authentic kinds of support teachers need to be their best selves. What is required for all of us to be our best selves? What can we do? Where's the connection to relational knowing?

If you go back into your memory and think of your very earliest first day of school memories, can you remember what you wore and how you felt? Do you remember wearing new clothes on that first day, or hand-me-downs? What kinds of shoes did you wear? What kinds of school supplies did you have? What were you thinking and feeling during those first few days of school? For some of us, there may have been new clothes and shoes, along with new pencils, a new backpack, and brand new crayons to go along with the butterflies in the stomach. For some, the anxiety of the unknown at such a young age may have brought on tears or even those tears that embarrassingly trickle down our legs.

Try to focus on your memories of your first teacher (possibly in kindergarten or first grade). What kind of person was that teacher and how do you remember feeling around him or her? Did you feel encouraged, supported, and cared for? Or, were you compared to others in a way that made you feel "less than"? Now, shift your attention slightly and focus on your very favorite teacher or class. How did your favorite teacher make you feel? What are some of your memories of being in that class with your favorite teacher? What was happening in the classroom of your favorite teacher?

When doing this kind of internal gazing down memory lane, all kinds of images may emerge, and it may be helpful to allow whatever emerges to marinate within you. However, if there was any kind of serious trauma that happened and you have not healed from that, spending time with a trustworthy counselor may be helpful so you don't have to suffer from unresolved pain that happened years ago. Such pain should not take any more space in your heart, mind, or life. It's possible that you took on tasks or witnessed some things that no child should experience, and it is only upon reflection that you realize this. This is particularly important for educators as we carry all of our life experiences and what we know about ourselves, others, and life with us when we take on the role of a teacher. Confront any unresolved pain or hurt, deal with it, heal from it, and move on! It is also important to realize that most people do the very best they can for who they are at every moment of time; extending grace to our younger selves and others can help!

Wide-Awakeness and Educators

You may wonder how all this reflecting about your earliest school memories is connected to relational knowing. As teachers, when we enter the "sacred space" of our classrooms, we bring *all* of us to that space—all of our embodied knowledge. While it's possible to think of a spectrum we are all on—from the side of "wide-awakeness" on the one end and completely apathetic, burned out, and "only there for the paycheck" on the other extreme—we might also consider ourselves as being part of a cycle with ebbs and flows, like the tide, or like a circular spiral slide on which we are constantly going up, down, and around. But to better understand either of these examples, let's start by looking at the extremes and link them all back together to relational knowing.

The notion of "wide-awakeness" as initially described by Alfred Schutz in 1967, a philosopher and sociologist, was later incorporated into the educational ideas of Maxine Greene (1977), who links wide-awakeness to our capacity and ability to take action, to *do* something, rather than to withdraw and take a passive stance to what we encounter. Even in the midst of the chaos and seemingly unbearable stress teachers encounter on a regular basis, Greene (2005) encourages teachers to "be awake, critical, [and] open to the world. It is an honor and a responsibility to be a teacher in such dark times—and to imagine, and to act on what we imagine, what we believe ought at last to be" (p. 80). Teachers' noble work focuses on a hopeful future and requires a deeply personal engagement and commitment to teaching. This passion and vow to stay engaged and "wide awake" involves conscious efforts to forge ahead with approaches to support students' growth and create meaningful lessons and activities, in spite of constant extra assignments and activities that seem to chip away from what we, as teachers, believe our students need the most.

One of the biggest obstacles is for teachers to be fully present, engaged, and "wide awake" to support their students to be their best selves. Teachers have the huge challenge to bring their best selves into the classroom, in spite of many personal issues and problems. For educators to be genuinely concerned about each and every student's growth and development, we oftentimes have to let go of our ego and focus on the students' needs. Our ego is the part of ourselves that is primarily concerned with our needs—above any and everyone else's needs. For egocentric educators, the focus is on "looking good" and having students who excel so the teachers or schools look good. The principal, Ava Coleman, in the contemporary television series, "Abbott Elementary," is hilarious in showing us what a self-absorbed egocentric educator looks like and does. The complex truth is that Ava is "both a villain and likable" (Ray, 2022), which often happens in all of our relationships, with all people, and within our own hearts and minds. What are the lessons we can learn from egocentric educators? On a regular basis, to be fully present for all our students, we need to scan our hearts to check who we're more concerned about—ourselves, our reputation, our interests, or our students?

HOW TO STAY PRESENT MOST OF THE TIME

If we are honest with ourselves, for most of us, thoughts flit in and out of our minds—with hummingbird-like speed. Research even suggests that teachers make an average of 1,500 decisions a day (Klein, 2021). Schools are actually places where there is an overabundance of organized chaos. So much is going on at every moment, and the teachers are tasked with creating engaging lessons to keep the chaos at bay. Internally, for teachers and students, a wide range of thoughts and feelings are constantly bubbling up. The current push to engage students and staff with social-emotional strategies provides practical approaches for everyone to maintain a sense of internal equilibrium that allows for more focus, teaching, and learning in the midst of the organized chaos all around.

Fundamentally, however, educators need to solidify our "why" to center ourselves on students' needs, with the hope that each and every student will grow and flourish. Our why serves as both the ballast in our ship and the rudder that steers the energy and activities. The ballast is the heavy material at the bottom of a ship to keep it stable and prevent it from capsizing. Like the ballast, our why is the deeply personal and philosophical reason why we teach. Do we genuinely believe that each and every child can learn and grow? Can we see the potential in each child or what they can become, beyond their current behavior or attitude? Do we recognize that we are all learning and growing moment by moment and have the capacity to expand our ways of thinking and being in the world? What are your fundamental beliefs?

How does taking time to really understand why we teach link to relational knowing? Current schools provide teachers with a lot of information and knowledge about students' scores, based on various local, state, and national tests. Additionally, former teachers of students often like to share with new grade-level teachers information they have on students, based on past experiences. There is also the in/famous "teacher lounge talk" where information is sometimes shared about students, even though such talk is often in violation of federal privacy laws, otherwise known as the Family Educational Rights and Privacy Act (FERPA). All of these sources of information might be sources of knowledge *about* a student, which is connected to relational knowledge. The knowledge or information about a student—whether in the form of a report card, standardized test, or from an administrator or another teacher—can become "fixed" in our heads and that knowledge can influence what we think about that student and how we might treat him/her. However, relational knowing is about having the courage to be open to form a fresh relationship with all students in order to get to know who they are and what is important to each of them. Relational knowing focuses on new possibilities beyond fixed ideas we might have developed about individuals or groups of students and taking action based on that openness to new information.

Whenever we encounter a person or a situation that is new to us, we naturally draw on the knowledge we have developed over time, based on our past experiences and/or interactions. Relational knowing, however, is about "suspending" that knowledge or information and making a conscious choice to start fresh with the person or situation in front of us. To be open to that person or situation and what we can learn from them—without the knowledge or information we have to "taint" us—is a huge, yet important, challenge for every educator. Since all students are in a developmental process of growing and learning—on the invisible, minute cellular level to the physical level— we must not allow ourselves to respond to students in a fixed fashion, based on prior knowledge. Every single day is a new day and a new opportunity to grow. Relational knowing centers on teachers wanting to make the effort and take the time to get to know students—what interests them, how they learn best, and what their dreams are for their future. Otherwise, we seek only to mold and shape students into who or what *we* think is best for them, without opening wide the door to possibilities for them to fully express their unique capabilities and fulfill their goals and dreams.

To develop the skill of embracing each and every child's clean slate of endless possibilities every single day requires us to have a heart open to new beginnings. How are we to develop such a spirit, which is central to relational knowing? One way is to strengthen our capacity to genuinely care for each student and have a mindset based on empathy. "Wait a minute!" you might shout. "That is not my role as a teacher; I'm here to teach xyz subject or grade; I'm not paid to care for all my students! It is their parents' job to care; I'm paid to teach!" Technically, you may be right, and caring for and demonstrating empathy for all students is probably not in a single job description. However, we know from Theodore Roosevelt and Rita Pierson that "students don't care what you know until they know that you care." Relational knowing is about caring to know your students in order to best support their growth. Greene (1978) emphasizes this very point when she tells us that teachers need to show up as "authentic persons living in the world, persons who are concerned—who care" (p. 48). A truly wondrous aspect of caring is that it can dramatically change situations that seem intractable. In fact, Agne (1999) suggests that "caring acts as leavening because a small amount may serve to cause expansion in each person encountered by it or engaged in it" (p. 179). Caring for another human being can change us and them!

Again, this may require that we step outside of our own needs and dig within to imagine what the student or person in front of us is going through, what their struggles are, and what we can do to walk together with them as they navigate whatever it is they are feeling and experiencing. It is not always about "fixing" the situation or coming up with a solution. Brené Brown (2018) clarifies the distinction between sympathy and empathy by reminding us that to be empathetic, we may need to imagine the same feeling of the person in front of us and just be present together with them—not offering a suggestion, solution, or critique. This is no easy task, especially for those of us who are full of suggestions and ideas to fix all kinds of problems! Relational knowing takes courage to be open, along with the capacity to suspend judging others for whatever they are going through; and it is about taking some kind of action, even if that action is to just sit quietly and be present in the silence.

EMPATHY AND CARE LINKED TO RELATIONAL KNOWING

A key aspect of relational knowing, then, is linked to our capacity to develop empathy toward our students, colleagues, and families. This can be extremely challenging at times! What to do? How can we feel empathy toward someone who is working our last nerve and irritates us to no end? To be empathetic, we must consider the other person's perspective and how they see a particular situation, even if it is very different from our own perspective. By intentionally seeking to be empathetic, we may be able to develop compassion—even toward those we dislike or disagree with on many topics. If we want to build bridges, rather than walls, this kind of uncomfortable work is necessary. Relational knowing is about having the spirit to persevere and persist in finding points of shared humanity. It does not mean we suppress our strong emotions or feelings with those with whom we have disagreements. "Rather, it is the realization that even those we dislike have qualities that can contribute to our lives and can afford us the opportunity to grow in our own humanity" (Ikeda, 2021, p. 7). This requires a deep dig within to acknowledge some very uncomfortable aspects of ourselves. What is it about that other person that irritates me so much? Is it possible that they are serving as a mirror to me to show me aspects of myself I don't like? These kinds of thoughts and questions push us to look at ourselves, rather than judge others. The challenge for many of us is how to suspend that judgmental voice.

If, for example, I am intolerant of intolerant people, am I not also being intolerant? The goal is to seek out and find the intersections of shared human-ity—losing a loved one, for example, or discovering a shared interest in spending time outdoors. Whatever it is, the goal is to have the courage to persist in connecting with that person. It is the connection that is the very first step in building any kind of relationship. We can choose to continue living in a divided world, or we can determine to find ways to connect with others, in spite of religious, political or ideological differences that may invade our thoughts as we engage with our students, colleagues, or students' families.

The compassion that can serve as a doorway to relational knowing must also be extended to ourselves. We were each born into, raised, and grew up in very different circumstances, and it is essential that we honestly reflect on ways our familial and school upbringing influenced how we see our-selves, others, and the world. When we look back on how we acted or what we said or did, we may realize that we said or did things that were hurtful or disrespectful. However, "developing self-compassion helps us to prac-tice authentic, open-hearted empathy and social perspective-taking during highly stressful, contentious situations" (Donahue-Keegan, 2021, p. 108). Essentially, we must extend grace, forgiveness, and compassion to ourselves while simultaneously remaining accountable for our actions. A beautiful and simple Hawaiian prayer, called *Ho'oponopono*, involves us repeating the fol-lowing to ourselves: "I'm sorry; please forgive me; thank you; I love you." Regardless of our religious faith and practice, this kind of private prayer of self-compassion can help us cleanse and expand our hearts to better connect with those around us by strengthening our beliefs in ourselves while working to forgive and love ourselves—even knowing we have so many flaws.

Finally, relational knowing is inextricably linked to our beliefs about equity and the unique beauty, talents, and value of every single student. Baruti Kafele (2021) suggests that "equity is not solely something that you do. Equity is who you are. Equity is a reflection of the educators' humanity toward the students they serve" (p. 18). When we ponder our "why" as an educator; when we do the inner work of caring for ourselves so we can be "wide awake" for our students, and when we challenge ourselves to care for each of our students' well-being, based on empathy and compassion, we are creating a space to relate to, connect with, and support each of our students. Teaching is a noble profession in which we have the potential to genuinely connect with our students in positive, uplifting, and meaningful ways. Relational knowing is about that click, that "magic" that can happen when each and every one of our students feels heard, valued, understood, and supported for the precious human being each of them is or is in the process of becoming.

REFERENCES

Agne, K. (1999). Caring: The way of the master teacher. In R. Lipka & T. Brinthaupt (Eds.), *The role of self in teacher development* (pp. 165–188). State University of New York Press.

Brown, B. (2018). *Dare to Lead.* Random House.

Donahue-Keegan, D. (2021). Social-emotional learning and value-creating education: Synergistic possibilities for cultivating hope and joy in education. In I. Nuñez & J. Goulah (Eds.), *Hope and joy in education: Engaging Daisaku Ikeda across curriculum and context* (pp. 104–113). Teachers College Press.

Greene, M. (1977). Toward wide-awakeness: An argument for the arts and humanities in education. *Teachers College Record, 79*(1), 119–125.

Greene, M. (1978). *Landscape of learning.* Teachers College Press.

Greene, M. (2005). Teaching in a moment of crisis: The spaces of imagination. *The New Educator, 1*(2), 77–80. doi: 10.1080/15476880590934326.

Hollingsworth, S., Dybdahl, M., & Minarik, L. T. (1993). By chart and chance and passion: The importance of relational knowing in learning to teach. *Curriculum Inquiry, 23*(1), 5–35.

Ikeda, D. (2021). *The light of learning.* Middleway Press.

Kafele, B. K. (2021). *The equity and social justice education 50: Critical questions for improving opportunities and outcomes for Black students.* ASCD.

Klein, A. (2021, December 6). 1500 Decisions a day (at least!): How teachers cope with a dizzying array of questions. *Education Week.* https://www.edweek.org/teaching-learning/1-500-decisions-a-day-at-least-how-teachers-cope-with-a-dizzying-array-of-questions/2021/12.

Miller, J. L. (1990). *Creating spaces and finding voices: Teachers collaborating for empowerment.* State University of New York Press

Ray, A. (2022, March 22). What makes principal Ava so funny on *Abbott Elementary? Harper's Bazaar.* https://www.harpersbazaar.com/culture/film-tv/a39454925/what-makes-principal-ava-so-funny-on-abbott-elementary/.

Williams, R. (2017). Being with and being there: Our enactment of wide-awakeness. *International Journal of Education & the Arts, 18*(21), 1–27. http://www.ijea.org/v18n21/.

Relational Cultural Knowing
Respecting Diverse Ways of Being

WHAT IS RELATIONAL CULTURAL KNOWING?

As human beings we have so very many ways that we are generally alike. Let us list the ones that immediately come to mind. Feel free to add things you immediately think of that we may have overlooked.

One nose	Two eyes	One species	Facility to think
One mouth	Two ears	Red blood	Facility to imagine
Two hands	Two hands	99.9 percent of our DNA	Facility to create
Two feet	Ten fingers	Experience emotions	Facility to learn
Two legs	Ten toes		

Of course, we've missed some, but the ways in which we are generally quite similar are quantifiable. However, the ways in which we as individuals differ are endless. For example (don't forget to add to the list):

Age	Thought process	Communication style	Socially acquired values
Style (aesthetic)	Skin color	Language	Socially acquired beliefs
Personality	Socioeconomic status	Dialect	Socially acquired practices
Ethnicity	Education	Experience	Rules of conduct
National origin	Religion	Hair texture	Family dynamics

Additionally, even the similarities listed above can represent superficial differences—I have two brown eyes but you may have two green eyes; someone may have ten long, piano player fingers while someone else has ten short, stubby digits; you might have an olive-colored, sun-kissed skin tone while your neighbor is fair-skinned or pale. And if we want to talk about how *groups* of human beings may differ from other groups of human beings, we could copy and paste much of what's in the list directly above. For example, groups of people share a language that is not the same language as another group of people; folks from Boston share a dialect that is very different from the dialect of people in Texas; various subcultures (Pang, 2018) like skaters, wine enthusiasts, Democrats or Republicans, wheelchair athletes, and so on share a specific style of dress, code of conduct, or way of thinking; people who are from the same race or ethnicity often share similarities that differ from other racial or ethnic groups; and so on. (Don't get sidetracked by the term *subculture*. Pang [2018] defines subculture as simply "a smaller community that has shared features that distinguish it from a larger social group" [p. 47]. So, like skaters, wine enthusiasts, Democrats or Republicans, wheelchair athletes, etc.).

So, let's think for a second. Are we truly able to get to know someone purely based on our similarities? If all you know about an individual or a group of people is that they have eyes, ears, a nose, and a mouth, and they are sometimes mad, sad, excited, or glad, do you really *know* them? If all you focus on about an individual or group of people are the surface-level differences, like skin color, style of dress, or speech pattern, do you really know them? In order to combat superficial knowing, we must acknowledge the powerful impact of culture on relationships and relationship building; we call this relational cultural knowing.

When we began to think about and research the influence of culture on connections between individuals, we became intrigued by relational cultural theory (Miller, 1976). Relational cultural theory "brings into focus the influence of larger culture and power differentials on the quality and nature of relationships and the subsequent effects on healthy coexistence" (McCauley, 2013, para. 1). Like relational cultural theory, relational cultural knowing recognizes the magnitude of cultural context to human development and relationship building. With this in mind, we define relational cultural knowing in the following way: *relational cultural knowing is understanding that culture powerfully impacts relationship and relationship building and therefore acknowledging and respecting cultural variety in our regard for and behavior toward one another.*

If we go back to our tunnel analogy (we like tunnels), consider that mostly all tunnels have an entrance and an exit, commonly at each end; so when you see a tunnel you know it's a tunnel by its appearance. The aesthetics at the tunnel opening may be quite inviting with flowers or foliage, or maybe a clear, unobstructed path. On the other hand, there may be "keep out" signs, weeds, or complete darkness before you. These external differences represent the surface distinctions masking the similarities and presenting an outward representation of our internal differences. If the external aesthetics are similar to our own, we may feel comfortable moving closer to the entrance. If it's very different from our own, we may be a little more hesitant to peek inside, even though we know it's still simply a tunnel. In other words, even though we know a person is a person, our differences—whether external and superficial or internal and significant—often keep us from moving beyond simple relational knowledge (see chapter 2). If we truly want to build relationship with another, it's imperative that we recognize how culture, in all its forms, directly influences how we engage with, communicate with, react to, show care for, and construct (or deconstruct) our knowledge of one another.

WAIT . . . WHAT IS CULTURE?

Before you read further, take a moment to write down how you define culture? What do you think of when you hear the word *culture*?

This was one of the top results of a Google search of "definitions of culture" (see figure 5.1):

https://www.yourdictionary.com › culture   ⋮

Best 44 Definitions of Culture - YourDictionary

Culture definition · The totality of socially transmitted behavior patterns, arts, beliefs, institutions, and all other products of human work and thought. · The ...

Figure 5.1   Google Search.

And forty-four is only the tip of the iceberg! There are literally hundreds of definitions for the word culture. Remember, we defined relational cultural knowing as *understanding that culture powerfully impacts relationship and relationship building and therefore acknowledging and respecting cultural variety in our regard for and behavior toward one another.* But how do we define that thing that powerfully impacts relationship and relationship building? What is that *thing*? It's any and all of the groups a person may belong to or identify with based on their outward and inward beliefs, norms, values, assumptions, language, appearance, behaviors, rituals, experiences, genetic predispositions, and choices and orientations. Every group that I belong to influences who I am, inside and out; and you can't cultivate an authentic relationship with me if you don't recognize and respect that my culture shapes the way that I see myself, you, and the world around us; and because your culture impacts you in the same way, our interaction—how we view one another and the way we work and play together—will be greatly influenced by our respective cultural backgrounds.

When African Americans talk about Black Lives Matter, and some who are not African American rebut with *all* lives matter, it's because they are not acknowledging the cultural impact that being Black in America has had on Black people. When a teacher who doesn't have attention deficit disorder tells a student who does, "all you have to do is focus!" it's because the teacher isn't acknowledging that those who belong to this group of individuals cannot simply focus this neurological disorder away. When a supervisor tells an employee who is Muslim not to take a break for prayer, the supervisor most likely doesn't respect the importance and significance of this religious practice to the employee's inner peace and personal identity. The Black Lives Matter advocate and the all lives matter proponent, the teacher and the student, and the supervisor and employee will not build successful, productive, caring relationships with one another without relational cultural knowing.

FOSTERING RELATIONAL CULTURAL KNOWING

Offering a tool without showing how to use it leaves the borrower misusing the tool and potentially making things worse, throwing it out due to frustration, or wasting a lot of time before figuring out how it works. It's also quite possible that the borrower finds a new way to successfully use the tool. So while we offer ways to foster relational cultural knowing, we hope that you research, refine, and reflect to find additional ways to develop relational cultural knowing. Nevertheless, our BRIDGES acronym (figure 5.2) may help you get started.

Be Humble

Like culture, the word humble has many meanings. We want to focus on the denotation of humble that simply says "not arrogant." Arrogance is an attitude of superiority. When we see ourselves as better than, greater than, and more important than, then we see those we're comparing ourself to as worse than, lesser than, and less important than ourselves. When we create this dynamic, we rob ourselves of the ability to appreciate diversity and differences as an opportunity for individual and collective growth.

How can you be humble to foster relational cultural knowing? There are so many ways to show humility, but this one will lead to so many others: acknowledge that your story isn't the only one in the book. So often, individuals who represent the dominant culture fail to practice cultural humility, which is the "ability to critically self-reflect on the existence of cultural differences and impacts on marginalized groups with the goal being to build relationships with those groups" (Brumley, 2020, para. 4). While this primarily refers to cultural differences represented by race and ethnicity, it can be applied when working to make a connection with anyone whose culture—in the broad sense of the word—is unlike your own. Cultural humility "fosters a way of

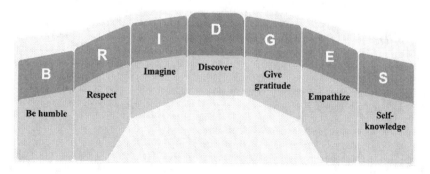

Figure 5.2 BRIDGES Acronym. *Source:* Author created.

thinking and knowing—a critical consciousness—of self, others, and the world" (Kumagai & Lypson, 2009, p. 783) that moves beyond the basic relational knowledge that sets everyone in rigid categories. Don't define the value of others based on some sort of imagined hierarchy that has you at the top.

Respect

Are you familiar with the 1986 Robert Fulghum book, *All I Really Need to Know I Learned in Kindergarten*? In it, Fulghum explains how the world would be a much better place if adults followed the basic rules children learn in kindergarten. A room full of kids would be chaos if they weren't taught and held accountable for respecting each other's person and property. A world full of adults can be and often is chaos because we often fail to show each other respect.

As you can tell throughout this book, we are big on definitions. With words that have multiple meanings, like culture, humility, and respect, if we don't clarify the meaning, then we lack a common understanding and may be prone to misunderstanding. So, the first definition several dictionaries list of respect involves feelings of admiration for someone or something; but The Britannica Dictionary lists the second definition of respect as "a feeling or understanding that someone or something is important, serious, etc., and should be treated in an appropriate way." That's the definition we want to focus on. Respect begins with accepting others for who they are, even when who they are is very unlike who you are. It's acknowledging that we each have a role in this story called life and every human being is a major, important, significant character in multiple storylines.

Imagine

Imagine that everyone you meet is simply a friend you haven't seen before. We're typically kinder to our friends and give them more of our time. We want to know everything about our friends—what they like, where they're from, what makes them happy, and what makes them sad. We find out how we're similar, and we let our dissimilarities pull us closer together as we explore them rather than allowing them to tear us apart.

Have you ever listened to all the lyrics of "Imagine" by John Lennon? We invite you to listen to that song or read the lyrics online and imagine.

Discover

Relational cultural knowing must involve a journey of discovery. If we are going to acknowledge and respect cultural variety in our regard for and behavior toward one another, then it's important for us to discover or become familiar with the variety of cultural and subcultural variances represented in our pluralistic society. Read, travel, ask questions, and pay attention.

Give Gratitude

The moment we shift our hearts and minds to a place of gratitude—for being alive, for breathing on our own, for having a roof over our heads and food to eat, for having people in our lives who love us and who we love, for those who have cared for us in the past, and so many other things—is the moment we embrace our lives and the lives of others. Having a disposition of gratitude can result in an instantaneous shift in how we relate to everything and everyone in our lives. Simply put, "gratitude has been linked with sleep quality, empathy, physical health, and emotional well-being" (Houser, 2018, p. 53). Scholars who have spent their lives studying gratitude (Emmons & McCullough, 2003; Portocarrero et al., 2020) recognize a clear link between having gratitude and one's well-being. The thing about gratitude is that it comes from within, and it is something we control—allowing us to experience it immediately. Our demeanor and mood change when we focus on what we can be grateful for at this moment, thus helping us and those around us when we have an attitude of gratitude. Ok. The rhyming scheme might be a little corny, but it is true! By sitting in a place grounded in an attitude of gratitude for the good and the bad in our lives, which have all served to help us grow, we can give ourselves and those around us huge gifts of well-being. Gratitude might very well be the "secret" key to happiness and expanding our capacity to embrace those from other cultures and what we can learn from them.

Empathize

Mistreatment, discrimination, or dismissal based on ability, race, ethnicity, age, gender, and so on, can only be fully understood by others of that race, ethnicity, age, gender, and so forth. For example, if you are forty years old now, even though you've been fifteen before, you've never been fifteen in this day and age, so you can't fully understand it when that teenager tells you about the constant peer pressure they face even though you likely also faced peer pressure in your teens. Social media has greatly increased the amount and the impact of peer pressure on teens. Additionally, if you are a person who is White and you've been stopped by a police officer, you can't fully understand when a person of color talks about their feelings when stopped by a police officer. But "empathy is not connecting to an experience, it's connecting to the emotions that underpin an experience" (Brown, 2018, p. 140). To show empathy, we must be open to multiple perspectives and accept that our way, our view, our feelings, and our experiences are not the only ones that exist or matter.

Self-Knowledge

When we spend most of our time around people who are similar to us, we tend to take our background and cultural behavioral patterns for granted. We may not even realize that our values, beliefs, and customs might be peculiar to someone else. But "if you think of your own way of life as the default and everyone else's as a strange variation, it's hard to approach those differences with respect" (unifrog). Consequently, one of the best ways to develop relational cultural knowledge is to examine your own cultural background. Below is an activity that may help you dive into your own cultural background.

Teachers have a great opportunity to develop self-knowledge through conducting a critical family history (CFH). CFH involves doing traditional genealogy work to explore your family's history, but with a twist. Chrsitine Sleeter (2016) "coined the term 'critical family history' to challenge family historians to construct their histories in the context of social relationships forged through colonization, racism, and other relations of power" (p. 14). What does this mean? Basically, you explore your family's history to acknowledge in what ways your family was either oppressed by others or was the oppressor and took advantage of others, or possibly a combination of the two. How did economic, racial, or political power in society impact your ancestors? In doing this kind of research within our own family narratives, we can critically examine events oftentimes ignored or brushed under the rug. This kind of project challenges us to explore family narratives.

Exploring your family's history through CFH goes beyond looking up names and dates of ancestors to include what their places were in the society at the time in history when they were alive. This kind of family research brings history alive and is a wonderful way to acknowledge how your family engaged with (or didn't) the many societal issues going on. Conducting a CFH gives you the chance to take an honest look at family stories you may have heard and/or ask some questions about how your family members honestly felt about people of other faiths, ethnic groups, or in any way different from your family. It can be enlightening and/or uncomfortable, but you are sure to face aspects of your family's history you may have never considered before (not with the intent of evoking guilt or assigning blame, but with the goal of understanding generational beliefs and practices that may impact our ability to build authentic relationships with people whose cultural background is different from our own).

Conducting a CFH requires us to have courageous conversations about our families and how we were raised. These are the kinds of questions to consider when doing a CFH:

- How did my family end up living here?
- What were their motivations to move here?
- What are some ways my family or ancestors thought about people different from us? Can I think of specific examples or comments made when I was growing up?
- What do I think would happen if someone in my family married someone who . . . ?
- What are some family stories nobody really likes talking about and why is that?
- What are some things we are really proud of/ashamed of as a family?
- How has our family dealt with issues of race, in the past and present?
- How does our family accept/embrace/reject family members who are LGBTQ+?

We've given you seven ways to foster relational cultural knowing. What are some other things you plan to do to better understand, acknowledge, and respect cultural variety in your regard for and behavior toward others?

WHY IS RELATIONAL CULTURAL KNOWING
IMPORTANT FOR EDUCATORS?

Students come to our classroom with a history. They are not empty vessels needing to be filled (Piaget, 1952). While they are still growing and developing (as are we all), they come with a wide range of experience, familial and cultural beliefs and values, and established attitudes and behaviors. What's more is that this history shapes how students learn. Pang (2018) makes the following assertion:

> The culture individuals have grown up with may have taught people different goals, and many teachers do not fully understand the diverse social contexts of their students. Research has shown that these cultural elements make a difference in how children learn. Teachers need to realize that their students may not have the same goals or cultural frames of reference as they have. Students may come to school with different cultural learning experiences. (p. 83)

When teachers respect the various cultures and subcultures to which their students belong, they can begin to develop cultural sensitivity and a semblance of what Milner (2006) calls culturally informed connections. Often the awareness and comprehension that arise from these efforts result in the assignment of worth and importance to the relationship, which leads to relational value (see chapter 6).

We would be remiss if we didn't explicitly talk about relational cultural knowing and the cultural divide between teachers and students as it specifically relates to race and ethnicity. Statistics assert that anywhere from 80 to 90 percent of the US public K–12 teacher population is White, and the student population is steadily growing more and more diverse (National Center for Education Statistics, 2022a; U.S. Department of Education, 2016). In fact, African American, Hispanic, Asian, Native American, and multi-racial youth make up the majority of the approximately 49.5 million students in the nation's public schools (National Center for Education Statistics, 2022b). Consequently, it's more important than ever for teachers to initiate and nurture relational cultural knowing between themselves and their students. When teachers are unwilling to acknowledge and respect their students' (and students' families) cultural variety, it leads the teacher to view students through a racialized lens that devalues the students' and their family's cultural identity.

Additionally, teachers, administrators, counselors, coaches, and other school leaders typically teach students how to function and "be successful" within the majority or dominant culture in society without addressing the importance of various individual cultural (and social) factors. When these contextual influences are ignored, there is a risk of perpetuating cultural misunderstandings.

REFERENCES

Brown, B. (2018). *Dare to lead.* Random House.

Brumley, J. (2020, December 16). *'Cultural humility' fosters a lifelong self-examination of racism.* Baptist News Global. https://baptistnews.com/article/cultural-humility-fosters-a-lifelong-self-examination-of-racism/#.YtrPJxPMKTc.

Emmons, R. A., & McCullough, M. E. (2003). Counting blessings versus burdens: An experimental investigation of gratitude and subjective well-being in daily life. *Journal of Personality and Social Psychology, 84*(2), 377–389.

Houser, K. (2018). Gratitude. *Leukos, 14*(2). doi: 10.1080/15502724.2018.1433934.

Kumagai, A. K., & Lypson, M. L. (2009). Beyond cultural competence: Critical consciousness, social justice, and multicultural education. *Academic Medicine, 84*, 782–787. doi: 10.1097/ACM.0b013e3181a42398.

McCauley, M. (2013). "Relational-Cultural Theory: Fostering Healthy Coexistence Through a Relational Lens." In Guy Burgess and Heidi Burgess. (Eds.) *Beyond Intractability.* Conflict Information Consortium, University of Colorado, Boulder. March 2013. http://www.beyondintractability.org/essay/relational-cultural-theory.

Miller, J. B. (1976). *Toward a new psychology of women.* Beacon Press.

Milner, H. R. (2006, Summer-Fall). The promise of black teachers' success with black students. *Educational Foundations*, 89–104.

National Center for Education Statistics. (2022a). Characteristics of Public School Teachers. *Condition of Education.* U.S. Department of Education, Institute of Education Sciences. https://nces.ed.gov/programs/coe/indicator/clr.

National Center for Education Statistics. (2022b). Fast Facts. *Back-to-school statistics.* U.S. Department of Education, Institute of Education Sciences. https://nces.ed.gov/fastfacts/display.asp?id=372.

Pang, V. O. (2018). *Diversity & equity in the classroom.* Cengage Learning.

Piaget, J. (1952). *The origins of intelligence in children.* W. W. Norton & Co.

Portocarrero, F. F., Gonzalez, K. & Ekema-Agbaw, M. (2020). A meta-analytic review of the relationship between dispositional gratitude and well-being. *Personality and Individual Differences, 164,* 1–14. doi: 10.1016/j.paid.2020.110101.

Sleeter, C. (2016). Critical family history: Situating family within contexts of power relationships. *Journal of Multidisciplinary Research, 8*(1), 11–24.

unifrog. (n.d.). *How to show respect towards people from other cultures: Learn to understand and appreciate people from every walk of life.* unifrog. https://www.unifrog.org/know-how/how-to-show-respect-towards-people-from-other-cultures

U.S. Department of Education. (2016). *The state of racial diversity in the educator workforce.* U.S. Department of Education, Office of Planning, Evaluation and Policy Development, Policy and Program Studies Service, Washington, D.C.

6

Relational Value
Creating Value in All Relationships

WHAT IS RELATIONAL VALUE?

Value is most often used as a noun, as in "the value of our relationship has no price"; or it can be used as a verb, as in "I value our relationship"; but it can also be used as an adjective, as in "she prefers the high-end products, while I seek out the best value products."

On the simplest level, we value anything or anyone we interpret as being important to us; we recognize the inherent worth of that person or object, and we seek to nurture or protect it, since we can acknowledge how precious it is to us. Within the relational realms, *relational value refers to the extent to which we honor, respect or appreciate those people, objects and ideas in our midst that we consider important.* Baumeister and Leary (1995) have long been engaged in studying the ideas and motivations linked to relational value, and they believe people are motivated by a need to belong, which can come from "affectively positive interactions within the context of long-term, caring relationships" (p. 522). In other words, we feel valued when we have a strong sense of belonging and feel cared for or cared about by others. Educators, then, hold the potential to foster a sense of relational value with students by developing caring relationships.

Ultimately, students feel valued when they are engaged in caring relationships with their teachers. The opposite of these feelings are loneliness, alienation, and rejection, which can have long-term deleterious effects, resulting in students feeling they don't "belong" in school. With so many potentially devastating negative impacts on students who are not engaged with caring teachers, we want to take a deeper dive into relational value and its significance.

Relational Value in Challenging Relationships

When we consider relational realms, we recognize that we have some kind of link, or relationship, with everything and everyone in our environment. We may have strong positive or negative beliefs, ideas, or opinions about certain people or ideas, and we may even ignore others; however, even those people or ideas we ignore or overlook are people/ideas with whom we are in a relationship on some level. To ignore, or, in effect, devalue something, puts us in a relation with them/it, albeit a negative one. Why is this important? As educators, we are in the position to *create* value, or to *find* value in each and every student, situation, and idea, if we frame our thinking to consider lessons we can learn from every single interaction, person, and idea. Considering lessons to learn in each interaction is part of finding its relational value.

Everything in life holds some level of value when we consider the growth potential behind the circumstance. We may be able to acknowledge its relational value when we ponder this quote below by Tina Turner:

> Everything and everyone has value, including experiences. Always keep the value from your experiences, especially what you learn from the negative ones, so that you may never repeat them. When I say *value*, I mean anything that enhances your life or serves your growth. It could be knowledge that you gained from an experience, or an inspirational memory of something you cherish. If it was a negative situation, or an interaction with people you'd prefer to forget, even if you cannot see any value in it, you can make a determination to never behave like the unpleasant people you encountered. That's valuable in itself. (Turner et al., 2020, p. 163)

This way of thinking shows us that we can potentially find relational value in each and every person and situation we encounter.

It is important to note that sometimes we hit roadblocks in discovering relational value because we spend too much time looking at what others are saying or doing *to* us rather than recognizing the golden nugget of valuable life lessons being presented in the midst of the relational dis-sonance (see ch. 3). Almost all educators can think of certain students, colleagues, or administrators in their lives that do things that irritate or challenge us, but those individuals can also be the very people who help us grow the most.

Authenticity is also important when seeking to find the value in a relationship. Brené Brown suggests that authenticity is a critical ele-ment needed for us to connect with others and find those places of shared humanity where all of us can grow, based on this idea of relational value. Oftentimes, the discomfort of our own inadequacies can be the obstacles that prevent us from connecting with others on meaningful levels so that we can get to the place of recognizing the relational value in an encounter or relationship. These real or perceived personal inadequacies may come from unresolved issues and act as obstacles to connecting with others, especially students. Brown et al. (2009) explain the link between authenticity and connectedness in relationships, stating that choosing authenticity means the following:

- cultivating the courage to be imperfect, to set boundaries, and to allow ourselves to be vulnerable.
- exercising the compassion that comes from knowing that we are all made of strength and struggle and are connected to each other through a loving and resilient human spirit; and
- nurturing the connection and sense of belonging that can happen when we believe that we are enough. (p. 368)

For educators, it is important to work on developing and paying attention to the delicate balance between being authentic, setting boundaries, and doing our own inner work to have the conviction that "we are enough." As we admit to ourselves our insecurities, imperfections, and vulnerabilities, we can develop the compassion and understanding to connect with our stu-dents, parents, colleagues, and administrators with greater empathy. This inner work is a pathway to connectedness and recognizing the relational value with all of those in our environment. Connecting with others through recognizing a shared loving and resilient human spirit is key and this is at the center of relational value. After all, we're all human and on the most basic level, we can find the relational value in our shared humanity through love, loss, suffering, and joy.

Relational Value as Linked to Schoolhouse Relationships

As we refer back to how we define relational value—considering *the extent to which we honor, respect, or appreciate those people, objects, and ideas in our midst that we consider important*—let's focus entirely on the various schoolhouse relationships and how an understanding of relational value can strengthen and even heal the many relationships contained within and around the school milieu. The last part of the above definition of relational value includes the phrase "that we consider impor- tant." Oftentimes, educators feel intense pressure to move the needle in terms of students' test scores and to ensure that all students are mastering the required curriculum objectives. While mastering curricular objectives is important, we suggest that educators must first and foremost focus on the relational realms with students and recognize the relational value in their relationships with each and every student they teach. This must be the starting point and the portal that leads to meaningful and substan- tive learning. We are suggesting that teachers consider fostering healthy and caring relationships with students as a key element that is at least as important as subject knowledge.

How will the lesson or interaction I have today with "Mary" contribute to her personal as well as academic feelings of accomplishment? Are there any changes I may need to make to support this student? What tone am I using in my interactions? How do I greet students and send them on to their next class or to go home? Do I send students away feeling encouraged and hopeful, or discouraged and dejected? What can *I* do to honor and respect each student? By, first, deeply reflecting on these kinds of questions and developing a genuine heart of care, we, as educators, can center our teach- ing on recognizing the relational value that exists when engaged with stu- dents. We can learn from our students just as much as they can learn from us, especially if we consider students' unique needs and situations in life. None of us is perfect, but by engaging in inner self-work to question our mindset, heart, and attitude, we can grow into the kind of human being and teacher we aspire to be.

REFERENCES

Baumeister, R. F., & Leary, M. F. (1995). The need to belong: Desire for interpersonal attachments as a fundamental human motivation. *Psychological Bulletin, 117*(3), 497–529.

Brown, B., Hernandez, V. R., & Villareal, Y. (2009). Connections: A 12-session psychoeducational resilience curriculum. In R. L. Dearing & J. P. Tangney (Eds.), *Shame in the therapy hour* (pp. 355–371). American Psychological Association.

Turner, T., Gold, T., & Curti, R. (2020). *Happiness becomes you: A guide to changing your life for good.* Atria Books.

7

Relational Spiritual Knowing
Soulful Connections

WHAT IS RELATIONAL SPIRITUAL KNOWING?

Before anyone freaks out, note that spiritual knowing is not in any way synonymous with religion. This will not be a chapter in which we try to convert you or get you to send us money for prayer beads. Spirituality transcends religious teaching or dogma and instead focuses on the human desire for internal and external harmony. In chapter 6 we talked about relational value; and if we allow ourselves to move even further beyond valuing the relationship to "discover the commonalities in human experience [creating] the opportunity for transcending differences, while honouring diversity in a complex and challenging world" (Gatmon, 2015), then we have ventured upon relational spiritual knowing.

But let's slow down a bit. What is relational spiritual knowing? We'll start with the dictionary, again (well, Google). Relational is defined as concerning the way in which two or more people or things are connected; spiritual is relating to or affecting the human spirit; and knowing is defined as showing or suggesting that one has knowledge or awareness that is secret or known to only a few. If we combine these, what we come up with is *the awareness of an inexplicable human connection between self and fellow human beings.* When we acknowledge that we are, each and every one of us, a part of a whole—an individual human being who is part of a larger human race—then we begin to experience human connection—that energy exchange between people who are paying attention to one another—and we begin to realize that no amount of differences should provoke us to harm (intellectually,

69

emotionally, mentally, physically) our fellow human being. It's like severing your own arm or leg or foot or ear. We are all connected.

Further in this chapter we talk about relational spiritual knowing in education, but let's return to the tunnel from chapter 3 for illustration. When we're traveling through the dissonance tunnel, it's dark. How does one move forward when unable to see past the nose on one's face? Whether we're in a familiar space or on new terrain, we have to move slowly and sense our surroundings. Relational spiritual knowing reveals to us the secret knowledge and awareness that the other person is also experiencing the darkness of the tunnel and if we work to "see" one another's position, together we can find our way to the light at the end. Relational spiritual knowing helps us through the dissonance because "it has everything to do with relationships that honor the soul, encourage the heart, inspire the mind, quicken the step, and heal the wounds we suffer along the way" (Palmer, 2018, p. 63). Ultimately, a core element of spirituality is learning to live in relationships.

OUR POSITIONALITY

A spiritual way of knowing is a central aspect of relational realms, but we want to explicitly re-state our belief that this in no way means that you must be religious to navigate the relational realms, and you do not have to be religious in order to be spiritual. Scholars, philosophers, and writers like Anzaldúa (2002), Buber (1967), Palmer (2000, 2018), and Koegeler-Abdi (2013) recognize the profound significance of spirituality in relational knowing and how it manifests in external appreciation for experiences with others that provide meaning and purpose (Wandix-White & Mokuria, 2021). Our goal through this chapter, through this entire book, is to offer a map for navigating relationships and analytical tools that provide theoretical and practical contexts for getting to the heart or root of positive relationship building in school environments and beyond. Nevertheless, relationships are personal. Consequently, it is inevitable in sharing what we've learned through our fifty collective years of education experience, innumerable hours of research, and over one hundred collective years of life that our positionality would seep through the ink on the pages.

Since positionality is a narrative that unravels and reveals life experiences that significantly influence one's perspective on a certain topic, for full transparency, we feel we should share a bit about our respective positionalities. We choose to share at this juncture because we both consider ourselves to be quite spiritual and for both of us, our personal spiritualities happen to be heavily rooted in our respective belief systems or religions. One of us is a Christian of unwavering faith, and one of us is a committed, practicing Buddhist. Within both belief systems, exhibiting love for others and working for the good of all mankind is a key concept, belief, and/or practice. It is this very basic and common belief that fuels our *awareness of an inexplicable human connection between self and fellow human beings* and cultivates our relational spiritual knowing.

Upon discussing spirituality, we wanted to get a third opinion from someone who would just answer a couple of questions and then let us get back to work. Notwithstanding the potential that they are spying on us and recording our every word, Alexa and Google Home can be pretty handy, always available third opinions. One of them led us to a Boston radio station website, WBUR, that had this to say about spirituality:

> What does it mean to be spiritual outside the confines of religion? For some, both exist side by side. For others, even those who consider themselves atheists or "nones," the concept of spirituality might feel critically important. They say it has to do with how we interact with others, with living more contemplatively, and with appreciating nature and the natural world. (Young & Miller-Medzon, 2020, para. 3)

The article goes on to say that finding ways to connect with individuals whose views differ from our own can be challenging; but, "ideally, the space where we reach out to one another is one where we don't allow our disagreements to define what's possible between us" (para. 11).

Take a moment to think about what your spirituality is rooted in and how it underpins your human connections or draws you toward the humanity of others. Completing the chart below (figure 7.1) might help get you started.

Is there a common theme in your answers (e.g., nature, reading/books, meditation, alone time, family time, creative expression, humor, exercise)? If a common theme is evident, you may have found the portal to your spirituality.

Chapter 7

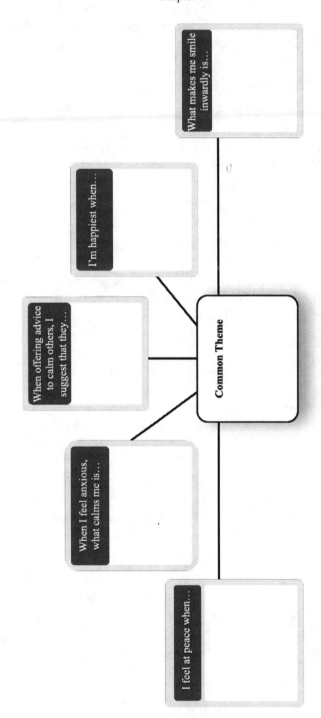

Figure 7.1 Roots of Spirituality Discovery Chart. *Source:* Author created.

RELATIONAL SPIRITUAL KNOWING IN EDUCATION

So, how does this intimately relate to the relationship between teacher and student, teacher and teacher, teacher and self, teacher and principal, and the host of teacher and ___ relationships in the schoolhouse?

When we speak of relational spiritual knowing and its connection to education, we are speaking of the deepest invisible roots of humanity and how educators can harness this type of knowing to support students' personal and academic growth and development, even—or *especially*—those students who are hard to get along with. This next sentence may be the "that's it!" clincher sentence that belongs at the end of this chapter, but we're going to drop it right here: opening ourselves to the deepest ways in which we make connections that transcend ephemeral experiences to embrace the shared human experience, leads to gratitude, empathy, patience, kindness, and compassion toward others. Boom! It's a spiritual way of knowing and connecting. When we tap into this relational spiritual knowing as educators, we may be able, for example, to demonstrate gratefulness for our colleagues, compassion toward our school leaders, kindness and patience with our students, and self-empathy.

In an online *Edutopia* article, Pete Reilly (2015) says if we are open to seeing our work as educators as not only a professional experience but also a spiritual one, we can use it as a mirror that reflects back to us what our students experience when they interact with us. He goes on to say, "[our students] reflect back to us our best qualities and our gifts, as well as the places where we don't quite live up to our own values and beliefs" (para. 3). Thus, relational spiritual knowing is very personal yet clearly palpable, making it a potentially powerful "tool" for educators to consider in their work. Following are three reasons:

First, a person's relational spiritual knowing is grounded in their personal, yet powerful beliefs about the very nature of life. For educators to recognize and harness their spiritual ways of knowing and understanding life and others, it is first essential to acknowledge the role of our ego and its connection to our spirituality. For most of us, our egos dominate how we live and what we do, with the primary goal being to prove that we are "right" and that our ways of knowing and being in the world are valid and meaningful. This need to be right is grounded in arrogance that often creates fissures in relationships because others can feel when they are being judged or criticized, even though we may work hard to hide those feelings. All of us are sensitive to being judged and criticized, and this is even more so the case with children who feel their teachers are judging them.

How can educators silence—even eliminate—that inner voice that is busily judging and criticizing students for a wide range of reasons? We want to encourage educators to draw on their core spiritual beliefs and link those beliefs to their initial feelings of being called to teach. Do you genuinely believe that each and every child is a precious human being worthy of great respect and kindness? Whether a child is in the "gifted" program or has so many physical and development challenges that s/he may never read or write, can you see that each child has a purpose or mission in this world and that as an educator, your role is to support that child's growth and development? Your answers to these questions will make a huge difference in how you teach, *if* you continue teaching, and whether or not you will be able to make meaningful connections with your students should you remain in the teaching profession.

If you do remain, you will inevitably encounter challenging relationships, and this is when you really have to tap into relational spiritual knowing, because teachers must maintain their professionalism and continue engaging with others they may consider to be challenging, whether those relationships are with a student, colleague or administrator.

A fascinating concept from the Buddhist tradition is called the reverse relationship, which can serve to help us understand how to find hope in those very relationships with students, supervisors, parents, or colleagues that are most painful, challenging, and may even cause us to consider leaving our beloved profession. When we are engaged with someone in a very negative way, we are still nonetheless in a relationship with them until we work through our own side of the negativity and resolve something within ourselves. Through that negativity, we may be able to grow and learn things about ourselves and others that we may not learn in any other way. Because of this, the very person or situation with whom we struggle the most can actually serve to help us grow in ways otherwise impossible; this is why it is called a "reverse" relationship.

Teaching entails so much more than disseminating knowledge, facts, and skills, and the teacher-student relationship is sacred because of the unique bond between teachers and students. For some teachers, the job is cut and dry: they are paid to teach a subject and they plan lessons and assessments to fulfill state requirements. Such teachers have a job, and their hearts are neither in their work nor in their students' well-being. However, by engaging in the kind of work we outline in this book, we are confident that all teachers can re-awaken to their missions and callings to support every young person in their classroom.

The second reason relational spiritual knowing can be a powerful tool for educators is because it encourages them to create a culture of care in their classrooms. Such a culture resonates with bell hooks' notion of "radical love," in which she unapologetically recognizes the link between education and caring for students' souls. For hooks (1994), "to teach in a manner that respects and cares for the souls of our students is essential if we are to provide the necessary conditions where learning can most deeply and intimately begin" (p. 13). As teachers, we can choose to consider relational spiritual knowing and find the space within ourselves to care for and honor each student as a spiritual sojourner in our midst.

The third way relational spiritual knowing can support educators is by providing an internal mechanism to prevent burnout. Much like the story made famous by Covey (2013) of "sharpening the saw," educators would benefit from anchoring their lives in some kind of spiritual practice that gives them inner peace, whether it is tied to a religion or not. To summarize the story of "sharpening the saw," a lumberjack was working incredibly hard to cut down a tree and refused to take a break to sharpen the saw; however, he eventually learned that by taking a pause to sharpen the saw, the tree-cutting process became significantly easier. Nurturing and tending your own spirit is much like pausing to "sharpen the saw" of your life.

When we exercise and eat healthy, nutritious food, we usually feel better because, on the most basic level, our cells are more fully oxygenated and can function to help each other to support our overall feelings of well-being. When we neglect our health, it is hard to fully live our lives with the same vigor and excitement that we feel when we are feeling healthy and well. The same is true with our spiritual health. When we pay attention to, honor, and nurture our spirits, we expand the possibilities to more fully connect with and engage with others on that invisible, yet palpable, spiritual level. Recognizing the many ways our hearts experience happiness, sorrow, joy, pain, peace, and conflict can serve as bridges to our relational spiritual knowing in our relationships with everyone around us, especially our students.

It all begins within, and it is just as important to take care of and nurture your spirit for your overall well-being as it is to care of your health and body in order to live to your greatest potential. How can you help your students reach their greatest potential unless you, too, are working to reach yours? How can we expect students to have self-control and reflect on their attitudes or actions unless we, too, look within? You might start by considering what you consider to be your spiritual truths, and what that means for you as an educator. What are some of your most fundamental beliefs about the children you teach? Do you genuinely care for each student's success, well-being, and happiness? If you do, how can you communicate those feelings and beliefs to your students? If you are holding onto any negative thoughts, feelings, or beliefs about any of your students, how is that helping you or them? What can you do to shift those thoughts, feelings, or beliefs to compassion for whatever they are experiencing in their own lives so you can better support them? As you grow, your students will too.

For educators, an understanding of relational spiritual knowing can expand your capacity to put your life into your work with even more verve for the reasons explained above and summarized here: (1) by focusing on your core spiritual beliefs and letting go of your ego, you can support each student; (2) through creating a culture of care you are able to find a way within to connect spiritually with each student; and (3) through taking time on your personal renewal through your spiritual path, you can prevent burnout.

WHAT MIGHT I DO NOW? WAYS TO STRENGTHEN RELATIONAL SPIRITUAL KNOWING FOR EDUCATORS

You've already taken the first steps to strengthen relational spiritual knowing by working to discover what your spirituality is rooted in. Once you make that discovery, you may better understand how you connect to people (and for educators, connecting to the people we call our students is vital). If, for example, you found that your spirituality may be rooted in humor, then you may live in relationships and feel connected to others through laughter or playfulness. So for you, getting to know a student may include lighthearted (yet, respectful and appropriate) banter that results in shared laughter, which is "an important part of the story of relationships" (Algoe, 2017). Let's look at how this might look in relation to the other relational realms (see figure 7.2).

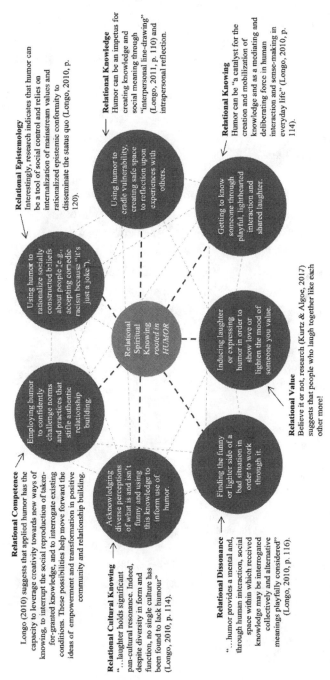

Relational Epistemology
Interestingly, research indicates that humor can be a tool of social control and relies on internalization of mainstream values and rationalized epistemic conformity to disseminate the status quo (Longo, 2010, p. 120).

Relational Knowledge
Humor can be an impetus for creating knowledge and social meaning through "interpersonal line-drawing" (Longo, 2011, p. 110) and intrapersonal reflection.

Relational Knowing
Humor can be "a catalyst for the creation and mobilization of knowledge and as a mediating and deliberating force in human interaction and sense-making in everyday life" (Longo, 2010, p. 114).

Relational Competence
Longo (2010) suggests that applied humor has the capacity to leverage creativity towards new ways of knowing, to interrupt the social reproduction of taken-for-granted knowledge, and to interrogate existing conditions. These possibilities help move forward the ideas of empowerment and transformation in positive community and relationship building.

Relational Cultural Knowing
"...laughter holds significant pan-cultural resonance. Indeed, despite diversity in form and function, no single culture has been found to lack humour" (Longo, 2010, p. 114).

Relational Dissonance
"...humor provides a mental and, through human interaction, social space within which received knowledge may be interrogated collectively and alternative meanings playfully considered" (Longo, 2010, p. 116).

Relational Value
Believe it or not, research (Kurtz & Algoe, 2017) suggests that people who laugh together like each other more!

Using humor to cradle vulnerability, creating safe space to reflection upon experiences with others.

Getting to know someone through playful, lighthearted interaction and shared laughter.

Using humor to rationalize socially constructed beliefs about people (e.g., accepting comedic racism because "it's just a joke").

Relational Spiritual Knowing rooted in HUMOR

Inducing laughter or expressing humor in order to show love or lighten the mood of someone you value.

Employing humor to confidently challenge norms and practices that stifle authentic relationship building.

Acknowledging diverse perceptions of what is and isn't funny and using this knowledge to inform use of humor.

Finding the funny or lighter side of a bad situation in order to work through it.

Figure 7.2   Relational Spiritual Knowing Rooted in Humor. *Source:* Author created.

You'll notice much of the verbiage on the graphic comes from an insightful study about humor in social work (Longo, 2010) which, like education, is a caring profession (Wandix-White, 2020) that must prioritize relationship building. However, it's very difficult to understand and appreciate others if you don't truly know and value yourself; and you can't connect to others on a spiritual plane if you don't even know where you spiritually stand. Consequently, the more you can work on your spiritual awareness, the more impactful you will be in your work with students, connecting with them in meaningful ways that support them on their own journeys.

We must briefly mention teacher self-care here because it is so intrinsically tied to relational spiritual knowing. Acknowledging and appreciating the nonmaterial qualities and experiences that provide purpose and meaning (Willis & Leone-Sheehan, 2019) has to start with self. Constantly reflecting upon, refreshing, and honoring the relationship we have with our own souls is essential to improving and maintaining our health and well-being. According to the National Institute of Mental Illness, there are six elements to self-care: emotional, physical, professional, psychological, social, spiritual. Tending to the spiritual, which is where we most often find meaning and purpose, will help you to know thyself and welcome growth and transformation into our lives as a whole. Okay, enough with the philosophy.

REFERENCES

Algoe, S. (2017, July 17). How laughter brings us together. *Greater Good Magazine.* (J. Suttie, Interviewer). https://greatergood.berkeley.edu/article/item/how_laughter_brings_us_together.

Anzaldúa, G. (2002). Now let us shift . . . the path of conocimiento . . . inner work, public acts. In G. Anzaldúa, G., & A. Keating (Eds.), *This bridge we call home: Radical visions for transformation* (pp. 540–577). Routledge.

Buber, M. (1967). *A believing humanism: My testament, 1902–1965* (Maurice Friedman, Trans.). Humanities Press International, Inc.

Covey, S. R. (2013). *The 7 habits of highly effective people: Powerful lessons in personal change.* Free Press.

Freire, P. (2012). *Pedagogy of the oppressed.* Continuum (Original work published in 1970).

Gatmon, A. (2015, May). Four ways of spiritual knowing: An epistemology for a diverse world. *Journal for the Study of Spirituality, 5*(1), 7–19. doi: 10.1179/2044 024315Z.00000000037.

hooks, b. (1994). *Teaching to transgress: Education as the practice of freedom.* Routledge.

Koegeler-Abdi, M. (2013). Shifting subjectivities: Mestizas, nepantleras, and Gloria Anzaldúa's legacy. *MELUS 38*(2), 71–88.

Kurtz, L. E., & Algoe, S. B. (2017). When sharing a laugh means sharing more: testing the role of shared laughter on short-term interpersonal consequences. *Journal of Nonverbal Behavior, 41*(1), 45–65. doi: 10.1007/s10919-016-0245-9.

Longo, M. (2010). Humour use and knowledge-making at the margins: serious lessons for social work practice. *Canadian Social Work Review / Revue Canadienne De Service Social, 27*(1), 113–126.

Palmer, P. (2000). *Let your life speak: Listening for the voice of vocation.* Jossey-Bass.

Palmer, P. (2018). *On the brink of everything: Grace, gravity, and getting old.* Berrett-Kelhler Publishers, Inc.

Reilly, P. (2015, September 14). *Teaching is a spiritual endeavor.* Edutopia. https://www.edutopia.org/discussion/teaching-spiritual-endeavor.

Turner, T. (2020). *Happiness becomes you: A guide to changing your life for good.* Atria Books.

Wandix-White, D. (2020). Caring and uncaring teacher practices: Examples from past offer guidance for present and hope for future. *Urban Education.* doi: 10.1177%2F0042085920914354.

Wandix-White, D., & Mokuria, V. (2021, April 8–12). Relational Realms: A Conceptual Framework [Conference presentation abstract]. 2021 Virtual American Educational Research Association AERA Annual Meeting. https://convention2.allacademic.com/one/aera/aera21/index.php?cmd=Online+Program+View+Paper&selected_paper_id=1689738&PHPSESSID=plh7rjbn9n2mk9rk3v4baas0l0.

Willis, D. G., & Leone-Sheehan, D. M. (2019). Spiritual knowing. *Advances in Nursing Science, 42*(1), 58–68. doi: 10.1097/ANS.0000000000000236.

Young. R., & Miller-Medzon, K. (2020, January 13). *Can spirituality exist without God? A growing number of Americans say yes.* WBUR Here & Now. https://www.wbur.org/hereandnow/2020/01/13/spirituality-krista-tippett.

8

Relational Competence

What We Aspire to Accomplish

We made it! You are here!

But that doesn't mean you'll always live here. Inevitably you'll rent some space in relational dissonance from time to time, your relational knowledge will trip you up and keep you from venturing out to foster relational knowing, and your anxiety regarding another culture will stop you from appreciating someone for who they are and building relational value. But here's the thing—noted psychologist Dr. Judith V. Jordan (2004) lists the following characteristics to describe relational competence:

- movement toward mutuality and mutual empathy
- noticing and caring about our impact on others
- being open to being influenced
- enjoying relational curiosity
- experiencing vulnerability as inevitable and a place of potential growth rather than danger
- creating good connection rather than exercising power over others as the path of growth

As long as we are *doing* these things—and notice that each begins with an action verb—then we are in the realm of relational competence.

As is our practice, let's formally define what we mean when we say relational competence. Previously, we defined relational as concerning the way in which two or more people or things are connected. The Oxford English Dictionary defines competence as the ability to do something successfully or efficiently. We also considered the other relational realms (epistemology, knowledge, knowing, cultural, dissonance, value, spiritual) discussed in this book as we came to a usable definition. Subsequently, we define relational competence as *the ability to effectively develop and sustain connection with another in a way that appreciates the uniqueness as well as the commonality of the individual's humanity and life experiences.* The information this book provides to aid you in navigating the other relational realms will help you grow in relational competence and strengthen your ability to build impactful, mutually respectful relationships. So if you started reading this chapter, hoping to get a magic relational competence recipe, you'll find that you need to go through the rest of the book to gather the ingredients.

Throughout this text, we have discussed navigating relational realms in various settings, but we always come back to the book's subtitle: *helping educators navigate and cultivate healthy schoolhouse relationships.* While we hope doctors and other medical personnel, leaders of corporations, police officers and other workers within the criminal justice system, social workers, spouses, friends, and anyone who is or desires to be in relationship with anyone else read this book and find it helpful in building and nurturing beautiful human connections, this chapter focuses primarily on helping teachers develop relational competence in their teacher-student relationships.

There are several other scholars and practitioners who offer insights into cultivating relational competence in the teacher-student relationship. We present and expound upon a few of them in the following pages.

Teacher-student relationships at the intersection of their divergent backgrounds have been a prominent issue in the United States for centuries. Over the last few decades, however, this phenomenon has become a prevalent international issue as "schools in South Africa, Eastern Europe, the middle East, Russia, and China are dealing with the dismantling of separate and unequal school systems to better integrate subordinate populations into the mainstream" (Ladson-Billings, 2004, p. 3). Scandinavian researchers Aspelin and Jonsson (2019) reference other Scandinavian research that states they are at a near consensus on how to define teachers' relational competence and that at the core of relational competence is the ability to "meet students and parents with openness and respect, to show empathy and to be able to take responsibility for one's own part of the relationship as an educator" (as cited in Aspelin & Jonsson, 2019, p. 265).

Much like traveling through the relational realms, meeting students and parents with openness and respect is at the heart of relational value. Showing empathy correlates with relational spiritual knowing and relational cultural knowing; while taking responsibility for one's own part of the relationship is relevant to how we're able to move from our foundational epistemology and knowledge to relational knowing. Additionally, we like that the word responsibility is used in this definition of relational competence. During a TEDx talk (Wandix-White, 2018), one of us considers the role of responsibility teachers have to their students. It's worth reciting here:

> What does it mean to be responsible? If you look responsible up in the dictionary, you may find phrases like, having an obligation to do something, or having control over or care for someone as part of one's job. Or my favorite definition of the word responsible, "being the primary cause of something and so able to be blamed or credited for it." . . . We, teachers, must accept some of the blame when our students are not successful. The children and young people placed in our care come from all walks of life. You may have a student who didn't come from a literacy rich environment. Didn't have anyone who could read to them, teach them to count to 10, or spell their name, or write their letters. At the secondary level you'll have students who have yet to have caring, responsible teachers and so they're struggling to keep up. At the moment that student becomes *your* student, whether he or she continues to plummet or begins to rise up is greatly contingent upon whether or not you care and take responsibility. You see we, teachers, are responsible for the academic achievement, intellectual growth, and social development of our students and we have to do whatever we can to help them succeed. And when you care and take responsibility and that student does succeed, be honored that you had something to do with that success. But when you don't care and you don't take responsibility, and your student fails to succeed, be willing to accept your part in that too. We, as teachers, have not only a unique opportunity, but also the immutable responsibility to support our students and help them along this journey.

So, as teachers, taking responsibility for our own part in our teacher-student relationships, and working to skillfully and empathetically navigate the various peaks and valleys these relationships encounter, puts us on the right path to positively impact our students both personally and academically.

WITH GREAT POWER COMES GREAT RESPONSIBILITY

"Being the primary cause of something and so able to be blamed or credited for it" implies quite a bit of power. Think about that. As human beings, we have the ability to influence how other human beings feel, think, and behave. Sure, we can say one only has the power the other allows him/her to have, but even if within ourselves we adamantly refuse to allow Aunt Shirley's snide remarks about our weight upset us, it still manages to get under our skin, if only for the briefest of moments. With such power, some education researchers (including us) believe that relational competence must be addressed in teacher preparation programs and should be part of the overall professionalism of a teacher. Jensen et al. (2015) and Juul and Jensen (2002) share this sentiment and define relational competence in the following way:

> The professional's ability to "see" the individual child on its own terms and attune her behaviour accordingly without giving up leadership, as well as the ability to be authentic in her contact with the child. And as the professional's ability and interest in taking full responsibility for the quality of the relationship. (Jensen et al., 2015, p. 206)

Teacher professionalism is the knowledge, skills, and practices a teacher must have in order to be an effective educator. Since we know from our own experience as educators as well as the plethora of research that supports the notion that the teacher-student relationship is at the heart of the learning process, relational competence, surely, should be included in the catalog of skill and practice a teacher must have in order to be effective.

IT'S WHAT WE DO

Let's dive deeper. As we stated at the start of this chapter, being relationally competent and exhibiting the characteristics of relational competence requires action. It's how we respond when we experience relational dissonance; it's what we do with any questionable relational knowledge we've consumed; it's how we express our relational spiritual knowing; and it's how we embrace relational cultural knowing. It's everything we *do*. We send a communicative signal every time we *do* or *don't do* that forms, reorganizes, or causes an adaptation of synapses in the brain. Ewe (2020) comments that social bonds are built, strengthened, weakened, or destroyed in every moment of contact and, thus, all human contact involves a constant building, maintaining and repairing of relationships.

Close your eyes and picture someone you really like or love who makes you feel happy and peaceful. We'll wait.

Okay, open your eyes and think about how you feel in this moment and think of a word to describe that feeling. Jot it down here:

_____

Now, take a deep breath, close your eyes, and picture someone who you dislike or who causes you much anxiety and stress.

Now open your eyes and think about how you feel in this moment and think of a word to describe that feeling. Write that word down here:

_____

Did you feel better and think of a more positive word the first time? Or did you feel better and think of a more positive word the second time?

There was a study conducted with 120 six-year-olds. They were sat at computers and asked to answer questions or solve problems based on material they'd previously been tested on and knew. Periodically, in between questions, a very quick picture of their teacher was flashed on the screen. So quickly, in a time span so brief that the children may not have even been aware of what they saw. It was very subliminal. But it had an effect! The children who had a close, affectionate relationship with their teacher, as opposed to a weak, distant, or negative relationship with the teacher, ended up solving many problems faster and exhibiting less anxiety (Ahnert et al., 2013). There is no getting around the fact that the relationship a student has with a teacher has a powerful bearing on the student's mental, emotional, and academic success. While we don't believe that any teacher enters the profession intending for their mere picture to cause a student to have a negative visceral reaction, if you're not intentionally working toward relational competence, you may be unintentionally demonstrating to your students that building relationship with them is unimportant to you and, subsequently, *they* are unimportant to you.

YOU MEAN I HAVE TO LIKE EVERYBODY?

Re-read the six characteristics of relational competence we listed for you at the beginning of this chapter. Then go through the chapter and read the definitions we offered—the ones we deduced and the ones from others who write about such things. What do they all have in common? They are all talking about actions, not feelings. Your foundational knowledge base (relational epistemology and relational knowledge) may spark feelings of antipathy toward a person or group of people, but your decision to be open to being influenced by new ways of knowing and connecting can help you interact with the person or group more effectively. Effective interaction doesn't necessarily equate to handholding while singing kumbaya. Getting to know someone through efforts toward relational knowing and relational cultural knowing requires a bit of relational curiosity and making an effort to get to know someone. Getting to know someone sometimes leads you to "feel" less enthusiastic about them, but you can still work toward mutuality and mutual empathy by examining your biases, looking at things from their perspective, and simply acknowledging that they are a human being, just like you are, who deserves to be treated as such, just like you do. It doesn't mean you have to like them, but showing them respect and consideration as a fellow human being demonstrates a certain level of relational competence. When you experience relational dissonance, you must notice and care about your impact on others. You can care about how you make another human being feel without feeling that you like that human being. As you work to cultivate relational value or search for relational spiritual knowing, you'll need to be vulnerable and reflective. You can find value in a person or relationship and discover a deep connection to them and still not *feel* all warm and fuzzy about them.

If you haven't already, you will inevitably come across a student or family that you don't particularly like. Yes, we said it. As teachers, we're often afraid to admit that we don't like a student or a student's family. We don't *feel* joy or contentment in their presence. They make us *feel* agitated, frustrated, anxious, and sometimes even nauseous; but when we stop focusing on those *feelings*, we can start concentrating on connecting and *doing* what must be done to enter the realm of relational competence.

REFERENCES

Ahnert, L., Milatz, A., Kappler, G., Schneiderwind, J., & Fischer, R. (2013). The impact of teacher–child relationships on child cognitive performance as explored by a priming paradigm. *Developmental Psychology, 49*(3), 554–567. doi: 10.1037/a0031283.

Aspelin, J., & Jonsson, A. (2019) Relational competence in teacher education. Concept analysis and report from a pilot study. *Teacher Development, 23*(2), 264-283. doi: 10.1080/13664530.2019.1570323.

Ewe, L. P. (2020). Enhancing teachers' relational competence: A teacher lesson study. *International Journal for Lesson & Learning Studies, 9*(3), 1–18. doi: 10.1108/IJLLS-12-2019-0081.

Jensen, E., Skibsted, E. B., & Christensen, M. V. (2015). Educating teachers focusing on the development of reflective and relational competences. *Educational Research for Policy and Practice, 14*(3), 201–212. doi: 10.1007/s10671-015-9185-0.

Jordan, J. V. (2004). Relational resilience. In J. V. Jordan, M. Walker, & L. M. Hartling (Eds.), *The complexity of connections: Writings from the Stone Center's Jean Baker Miller Training Institute* (pp. 28–46). The Guilford Press.

Juul, J., & Jensen, H. (2002). *Pedagogical relational competence.* Copenhagen, DK: Apostrof.

Ladson-Billings, G. (2004). Landing on the wrong note: The price we paid for Brown. *Educational Researcher, 33*(7), 3–13.

Oxford English Dictionary (online). https://www.oed.com/view/Entry/221253?rskey=Gj0TBr&result=1#eid.

Wandix-White, D. (2018, May) *C.A.R.E: Calling all responsible educators* [Video]. TED Conferences https://www.ted.com/talks/diana_wandix_white_c_a_r_e_calling_all_responsible_educator.

9

Relational Realms as a Conceptual Tool for Scholarly Research

AN ANALYTICAL TOOL

There is a disconnect between teachers and researchers. That's not really a secret. The educators involved in the daily practice of teaching don't usually have time to sift through volumes of research or sit and decipher the loquacious renderings of education researchers. And the researchers and scholars who conduct education studies don't always have the time to navigate the red tape that allows them access to teachers and their students. As a result, there are a great amount of wonderful classroom practices that aren't getting shared with the masses, and there are a plethora of great ideas and proven practices written up in research documents that are never seen by more than a dozen or so practitioners. This chapter is written to offer teachers who want to conduct research about their engagement with students and researchers who study teacher-student relationship, a conceptual framework that makes it easier to analyze and verbalize the relational journey between teachers and students, and teachers and the host of others they encounter as educators.

We propose *relational realms* as a conceptual framework—an analytical tool that offers context for the exploration of positive teacher-student relationship building. As a conceptual framework, relational realms is rooted in the contention that teacher-student relationships consist of various internal and external ways of knowing and being that constantly and interactively release and retrieve energy which, when acknowledged and worked through, can result in authentic relationships that produce more effective teachers and maximize student outcomes.

Teacher-student relationships lie at the heart of the learning process. The growth culture created by positive teacher-student rapport has been associated with student outcomes, suggesting that putting relationship and responsibility before content and curriculum and over politics and prejudice is critical to student success. Over the last decade, considerable research has highlighted the importance of the teacher-student relationship to maximize the potential for academic and personal growth and development of students of color, in particular. The surge of research in this area comes as the US student population grows increasingly diverse, yet the teacher pool remains more than 80 percent White. The broad consensus within the literature is that educators must be equipped with the skills necessary to initiate, develop, and sustain authentic relationships with their diverse student body; not only for the sake of students but also for the overall well-being and effectiveness of the teacher. The major roadblocks to such relationships are not only external—cultural mismatch, socioeconomic differences, and life experience—but also internal, involving self-reflective practices that foster an inner peace that creates a more authentic self which, ultimately, makes external relationships more meaningful. While scholars recognize the importance of positive schoolhouse relationships, especially the teacher-student relationship, and some point out specific behaviors and practices that can encourage such relationships, scholarship that discusses the relational stages that lead to genuine relationships is often neglected. Thus, we offer an analytical tool that offers context for the exploration of positive teacher-student relationship building.

Let us note here that while our focus in this book is on relational realms in the schoolhouse setting, we posit that scholars and researchers in the fields of social work, health professions education (HPE), criminal justice, and many other disciplines could easily adapt the ideas presented here and use the relational realms conceptual framework in their studies and analyses. In an article on HPE by Varpio et al. (2020) that explores the ways theory, theoretical frameworks, and conceptual frameworks support each other, we can see how scholars who study a wide range of other relational issues can incorporate what we propose in this book.

Like the relational conceptual framework for multidisciplinary health research presented by Coen et al. (2010), our model "operates under the assumption that structures need not necessarily be material in nature to exert concrete consequences" (p. 4). In fact, the *relational realms* we present are

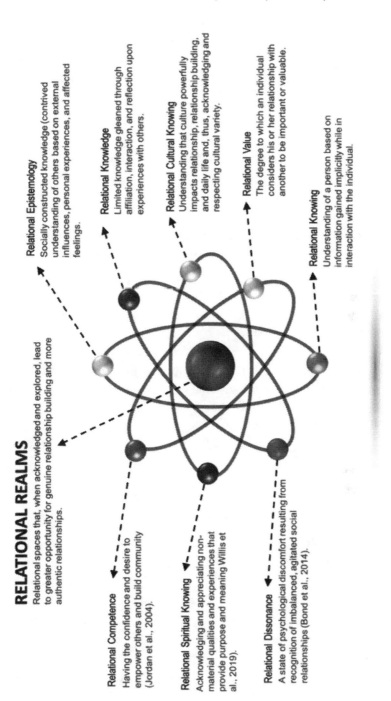

RELATIONAL REALMS

Relational spaces that, when acknowledged and explored, lead to greater opportunity for genuine relationship building and more authentic relationships.

Relational Epistemology
Socially constructed knowledge (contrived understanding of others based on external influences, personal experiences, and affected feelings.

Relational Knowledge
Limited knowledge gleaned through affiliation, interaction, and reflection upon experiences with others.

Relational Cultural Knowing
Understanding that culture powerfully impacts relationship, relationship building, and daily life and, thus, acknowledging and respecting cultural variety.

Relational Value
The degree to which an individual considers his or her relationship with another to be important or valuable.

Relational Knowing
Understanding of a person based on information gained implicitly while in interaction with the individual.

Relational Competence
Having the confidence and desire to empower others and build community (Jordan et al., 2004).

Relational Spiritual Knowing
Acknowledging and appreciating non-material qualities and experiences that provide purpose and meaning Willis et al., 2019).

Relational Dissonance
A state of psychological discomfort resulting from recognition of imbalanced, agitated social relationships (Bond et al., 2014).

Figure 9.1 Relational Realms as a Conceptual Framework. *Source:* Author created.

often intangible, and yet the exploration of these realms in the context of authentic teacher-student relationship building is vital (see figure 9.1).

As presenting a conceptual framework involves laying out the key factors or variables of the framework, and presenting the relationship among them, here we present one way in which relational realms flow. However, we acknowledge the fluidity of the relational realms and the existence of other manners of interactivity.

Relational epistemology (Thayer-Bacon, 1997, 2010) identifies knowing as a process through which individuals develop a pseudo-relationship with others based on socially constructed insight and/or superficial experiences with individuals or groups who create for the individual a synecdoche representing the entire group. This is dangerous in the teacher-student relationship, as both may view the other in accordance with similar others with whom they have interacted. Typically, this does not work out well for the student of color as teachers often report higher levels of negativity in their relationship with students of color, especially African American students (Murray et al., 2016; Wandix-White, 2020). While relational epistemology may provide "a sense of how interconnected we all are" (Lim, 2015, p. 15), these connections are often on the surface level and distorted. In order to combat this superficial knowing, a move toward relational knowledge is essential.

Relational knowledge involves an attempt to venture out past the shallow waters to a deeper understanding by reflecting on past interactions and investigating previous information in an effort to better comprehend others' feelings and patterns of behavior. Of course, it is difficult to gain such understanding if one does not acknowledge the powerful impact of culture on relationships and relationship building.

Thus, relational cultural knowing recognizes the significance of cultural context to relationship building. As outlined in chapter 5, when teachers acknowledge and respect the various cultures and social groups to which their students belong, they can begin to develop cultural sensitivity and practice culturally responsive teaching (Gay, 2010; Ladson-Billings, 1995). The resulting recognition and understanding often lead to the assignment of significance to the relationship, which leads to relational value.

Central to education is the idea that teachers know more than their students, but these unavoidable power dynamics can lead teachers to believe students and their voices are less valuable in the classroom setting. Not valuing students' funds of knowledge and contributions to the teaching and learning process creates barriers to building mutually respectful, value-ladened relationships. As value is synonymous with words like worth, importance, and regard, it is clear that in connection to teacher-student relationships, relational value is key to accessing the other relational realms. If we fail to value the presence, experiences, culture, and humanity of others, we will likely have no motivation to explore the various ways of knowing, being, and interacting that constitute the sum of the relational realms.

If relational epistemology is akin to reading a book about someone, and relational knowledge is then putting oneself in proximity to that individual and being mindful of our subsequent reactions; and relational cultural knowing subsequently involves paying attention to and respecting the cultural differences influencing our reactions; followed by relational value which emerges as the catalyst to work toward authentic relationship, then relational knowing is the logical next step. It is difficult, if not impossible, to realistically assign value to a teacher-student relationship if there has been no direct, implicit interaction between the teacher and student. Relational knowing—understanding a person based on information gained implicitly while interacting with the individual—can only occur when teachers take time to "get to know students." While a common culture, background, life choices, and interests may be shared by groups of people, each person is an individual, and building an authentic relationship with someone involves awareness of some of those idiosyncrasies that make one unique.

Sometimes relational knowing can prompt tension, conflict, or devaluation that results in relational dissonance (Bond et al., 2014). It is important for teachers to not allow relational dissonance to negatively influence their relationship with a student. It may be difficult for teachers to muddle through relational dissonance with students, but successfully traversing this realm is vital to the success of both the student and the teacher. Traversing this realm requires connecting to our inner realm of relational spiritual knowing.

A spiritual way of knowing is a very important component of relational realms. As pointed out in chapter 7, many scholars, philosophers, and writers recognize the profound significance of spirituality in relational knowing. Again, this does not mean one must be religious to navigate the relational realms. It warrants repeating that spirituality transcends religious teaching or dogma and instead focuses on the human soul and internal peace that manifest in external appreciation for non-material qualities and experiences that provide meaning and purpose.

No matter how the journey progresses or in what order the relational realms appear for each teacher, the end goal is relational competence (Jordan, 2004). Relational competence "occurs within a context of wishing to empower others and appreciating the life-giving nature of community building" (p. 15). Ultimately, a teacher's desire to empower students suggests the teacher believes in a relational epistemology and possesses relational knowledge that respects relational cultural knowing, values teacher-student relationships, works to build those relationships through relational knowing, acknowledges and works through relational dissonance, and engages often in critical self-reflection to cultivate their own relational spiritual knowing. All of this results in the movement toward mutuality and mutual empathy, noticing and caring about our impact on others, being open to being influenced, enjoying relational curiosity, experiencing vulnerability as inevitable and a place of potential growth rather than danger, and creating positive connection rather than exercising power over others as the path of growth.

Ultimately, relational realms offer a conceptual framework for scholars to use when researching the complex phenomenon of teacher-student relationships. It is our hope that scholars and practitioners find this to be an applicable and adaptable analytical tool to study, understand, and develop positive, authentic teacher-student relationships.

REFERENCES

Bond, L., Lusher, D., Williams, I., Butler, H. (2014, February). Friends or foes? Relational dissonance and adolescent psychological wellbeing. *PLoS ONE, 9*(2), e83388. Doi: 10.1371/journal.pone.0083388.

Coen, S. E., Bottorff, J. L., Johnson, J. L., & Ratner, P. A. (2010). A relational conceptual framework for multidisciplinary health research centre infrastructure. *Health Research Policy and Systems, 8*(29), 1–10.

Gay, G. (2010). *Culturally responsive teaching: Theory, research, and practice.* Teachers College Press.

Jordan, J. V. (2004). Toward competence and connection. In J. V. Jordan, M. Walker, & L. M. Hartling (Eds.), *The complexity of connection: Writings from the Stone Center's Jean Baker Miller Training Institute* (pp. 11–27). The Guilford Press.

Ladson-Billings, G. (1995). Toward a theory of culturally relevant pedagogy. *American Research Journal, 32*(3), 465-491. Doi: 10.3102/00028312032003465

Lim, L. (2015). Critical thinking, social education and the curriculum: Foregrounding a social and relational epistemology. *The Curriculum Journal, 26*(1), 4–23. Doi: 10.1080/09585176.2014.975733.

Miller, J. B. (1976). *Toward a new psychology of women.* Beacon Press.

Murray, C., Kosty, D., & Hauser-McLean, K. (2016). Social support and attachment to teachers: Relative importance and specificity among low-income children and youth of color. *Journal of Psychoeducational Assessment 34*(2), 119–135. Doi: 10.1177/0734282915592537.

Pang, V.O. (2018). *Diversity and equity in the classroom.* Cengage Learning.

Thayer-Bacon, B. (1997). The nurturing of a relational epistemology. *Educational Theory, 47*(2), 239–260.

Thayer-Bacon, B. (2010). A pragmatist and feminist relational epistemology. *European Journal of Pragmatism and American Philosophy, 2*(1), 1–22.

Varpio, L., Paradis, E., Uijtdehaage, & Young, M. (2020). The distinctions between theory, theoretical framework, and conceptual framework. *Academic Medicine, 95*(7), 989–994. doi: 10.1097/ACM.0000000000003075.

Wandix-White, D. (2020, April 4). Caring and uncaring teacher practices: Examples from past offer guidance for present and hope for future. *Urban Education, 0*(0) doi: 10.1177?2F0042085920914354.

Final Thoughts on Relational Realms

There is nothing new under the sun (Ecclesiastes 1:9). While we have named or "discovered" *relational realms*, we humbly recognize that what we've really done is engaged with and been in dialogue with the ideas and writings of the many scholars we've named throughout this book. We know that Sir Isaac Newton did not "discover" gravity; rather, he named a phenomenon that is part of our lives and impacts us all. And in Newton's naming of this phenomenon, we have a better understanding of how life works. Similarly, we feel that we are naming a phenomenon that is already part of our lives. Without a mirror, we cannot see the eyebrows on our faces so close to our eyes; we need the tool of the mirror to see something so close to us. Ideas circulate throughout the universe, and we build on the ideas of others; we always have and always will. In essence, countless predecessors guided us to explore relationships to acknowledge how we connect to others, which is a critical and central aspect of our lives.

In the current iteration of exploring relationships and the myriad ways we are all connected to each other, much like a kaleidoscope or spider's web, we envision a collaborative model that is both a lens of understanding and an analytical tool to give clarity about the complex relationships we have with ourselves and each other. Our hope in writing this book is to offer a fresh, new way of looking at ourselves and our relationships. Whether we want to strengthen the climate and culture of our homes, our classrooms, our schools, or our communities, we can benefit from looking at relational realms and how we connect with each other. This labor of love to formulate these ideas and write this book can be likened to cooking a lasagna. While we have a recipe and gather all the ingredients for our special dish, we also add a bit of this or a dash of that to make it all our own.

For this reason, we imagine future educators and scholars will build on the ingredients in our current "recipe" of relational realms and take these ideas to a level we cannot even conceive or imagine. Our hope for this book is that teachers, medical professionals, social workers, and others are able to use the lessons from this book to better understand relationships in their lives, especially those that are challenging or problematic. We attempt to describe a model *and* a process to navigate relationships as we all work toward relational competence.

Finally, we walk alongside you through the relational realms and though we know what we should and could do to successfully navigate them, we, too, stumble, get stuck, and have to constantly self-reflect as well as turn away from the mirror to selflessly gaze upon others in order to do the work that brings us into relational competence. This idea that it takes work and intentionality to get to relational competence and continued work and intentionality to stay in relationship competence is one of the key points of this book that we want you to remember.

Even as we ponder our own relationship, we're amazed at how often we find ourselves working through relational dissonance, holding each other accountable to acknowledge and address some of our flawed relational epistemology or relational knowledge, helping one another to see the other's perspective through our divergent cultural backgrounds, or realizing new relational value after digging deep within our spirits to get over disagreement. We constantly seek to build community with one another beyond our differences (Gumbs, 2020). The epilogue to an article we wrote together (Wandix-White & Mokuria, 2022) notes that we are two women who are

> so different from each other (Black/White, Christian/Buddhist, married/single, introvert/extrovert, intentional/spontaneous, reserved/exuberant, methodical/nonlinear) and yet so similar (brave/adventurous, right-brained, widowed at a young age, curious, intellectual, love of teaching and learning, mischievous, devoted mothers, educators, writers, and lovers of life) that the cyclical push and pull of our inevitable friendship often sparks creative and academic collaborative scholarship. (p. 8)

We hope that the present collaborative work inspires you to build the bridges that connect you to others in authentic and healthy ways, while living life as your best version of yourself.

REFERENCES

Gumbs, A. P. (2020). *Undrwoned: Black feminist lessons from marine mammals.* AK Press.

Wandix-White, D., & Mokuria, V. (2022). The time of our lives: Sick, sordid, cyclical. *Equity & Excellence in Education.* doi: 10.1080/10665684.2021.2021667.

About the Authors

Diana Wandix-White is an assistant professor of multicultural education at the University of Houston–Clear Lake. She completed her PhD in curriculum and instruction with an emphasis in urban education at Texas A&M University. Her research examines the impact of culture on the communication of care at the intersection of equity pedagogy, and the effect a classroom culture *of* care has on student growth and development. Dr. White's studies have been published in various scholarly journals, including *Urban Education, Equity & Excellence in Education*, and the *Journal of African American Women and Girls in Education*. Her methodological focus on narrative inquiry, both autobiographical and externally focused, has resulted in publication in the *Journal of Social Studies Education Research*, the *Journal of Curriculum Studies Research*, the *Journal of Interdisciplinary Studies in Education*, and the *Journal of Autoethnography*. Dr. White has also shared her work through multiple book chapters and a TED Talk.

Vicki G. Mokuria is an adjunct faculty member at Stephen F. Austin State University in Nacogdoches, Texas, in the Department of Education Studies. She completed her PhD in curriculum and instruction at Texas A&M University in College Station. Her research includes antiracism education, multicultural education, and Soka/value-creating education in Brazil. Dr. Mokuria studies teacher-student relationships in a wide range of contexts, with a specific focus on ways teachers' socialization and upbringing influence their interactions and attitudes toward their students. Dr. Mokuria's writings have been published in the following peer-reviewed journals: *Equity and Excellence in Education*, the *Journal of Interdisciplinary Studies in Education*, the *Journal of Social Studies Education in Research*, the *Journal of Faith, Education and Community*, and *Genealogy*. Her methodological approach is qualitative, specifically focusing on narrative inquiry and collaborative/auto-ethnographic work. Dr. Mokuria coauthored a chapter, "Narrative Inquiry as a Relational Methodology," which is in a book on narrative methodologies titled *Conceptual Analyses of Curriculum Inquiry Methodologies*. She has also coauthored chapters in two books currently in the publication process: *Toward Critical Multimodality* and *Value Creating Education: Teachers' Perceptions and Practice*.